KABBALAH

FOR HEALTH & WELLNESS

About the Author

Mark Stavish has over a quarter-century of experience in traditional spirituality and is an internationally respected authority in the study and practical application of alchemy, Kabbalah, and astrology. Stavish has published several hundred articles, book reviews, and interviews on the traditions of Western esotericism, many of which have been translated into numerous languages. He has also been a consultant to print and broadcast media as well as several documentaries.

In 1998, Stavish established the Institute for Hermetic Studies. In 2001, to further the advancement of nonsectarian and academic approaches to Western esotericism, he established the Louis Claude de St. Martin Fund, thereby creating the only widely known tax-deductible, nonprofit fund dedicated exclusively to advancing the study and practice of Western esotericism.

Stavish's education includes two undergraduate degrees, in theology and communications, and a master's degree in counseling. He has also been a member and officer in several traditional initiatic organizations focusing on Rosicrucianism, Martinism, and regular Freemasonry.

For more information on the Institute for Hermetic Studies and its program of activities and to receive its free electronic newsletter, *VOXHERMES*, visit its website at www.hermeticinstitute.org.

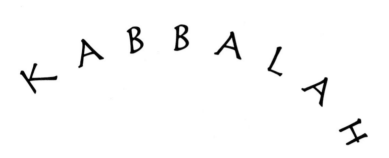

KABBALAH

FOR HEALTH & WELLNESS

MARK STAVISH

Llewellyn Publications
Woodbury, Minnesota

First Edition
First Printing, 2007

Book design and layout by Joanna Willis
Cover design by Kevin R. Brown
Cover hand image © Digitalvision
Interior illustrations by Llewellyn art department

Llewellyn is a registered trademark of Llewellyn Worldwide, Ltd.

Library of Congress Cataloging-in-Publication Data
Stavish, Mark, 1964–
   Kabbalah for health & wellness / Mark Stavish. — 1st ed.
     p. cm.
   Includes bibliographical references and index.
   ISBN-13: 978-0-7387-0977-2
   ISBN-10: 0-7387-0977-8
   1. Cabala. 2. Cabala—Health aspects. 3. Medicine, Magic, mystic, and spagiric.
4. Spiritual healing. 5. Mental healing. 6. Hermetism. 7. Occultism. I. Title.
II. Title: Kabbalah for health and wellness.

BF1623.C2S73 2007
133'.47—dc22   2006048801

Llewellyn Publications
A Division of Llewellyn Worldwide, Ltd.
2143 Wooddale Drive, Dept. 0-7387-0977-8
Woodbury, MN 55125-2989, U.S.A.
www.llewellyn.com

Printed in the United States of America

This book is dedicated to my wife and children,
and to all who seek to remove human ignorance and suffering
through the Kabbalistic Path.

Also by Mark Stavish

The Path of Alchemy

Contents

Exercises, Techniques, and Practices

Acknowledgments

Special thanks to the following, without whose generous assistance in time, talent, and treasure, this book would not have been possible: Christopher Bilardi, Paul Bowersox, Susan B. Layne, Dr. Don Melchior, Dr. Andrea M. Nerozzi, Carl Weschcke, Lisa Finander, and the staff of Llewellyn Publications—and above all, to the students, adepts, and masters of the traditions who have each added in their own way to the continual advancement of the Great Work.

Foreword

Whether we realize it or not, we are all participants in the evolution of awareness. Some of us pursue this as a noble undertaking worthy of daily practice and great effort. Others are happy to let the universe wash over them, experiencing a kind of cosmic erosion in which personal experience, ill health, and adversity work together to uncover an authentic self encouraged to awaken in the process. The only difference between these two groups is that the former actively promotes this natural evolution, acting to free and empower awareness, while the latter allows circumstance to work its glacial magic on their sleepy and submissive souls.

This excellent book by Mark Stavish is for those who wish to be an engaged participant. In fact, if you consider yourself a member of this group of seekers, *Kabbalah for Health & Wellness* may be the tool you have been looking for.

In my practice as a psychotherapist and shamanic practitioner, I am constantly presented with people who are looking for answers. Like most seekers in the postmodern world, they have found traditional faiths comforting, albeit short on substance, but feel very deeply that there is something more. They end up casting about, trying to find that thing all seekers are endeavoring to capture—enlightened awareness.

They read and listen and learn. They attend seminars and sermons, ritual meetings and drum circles. They get attunements, adjustments, and blessings. Having done so, they find that sometimes these experiences leave them stumbling around in a waking dream state or a trance state. Other times they may find themselves inexplicably in the non-dual causal, where communication with the outside world is difficult if not impossible, being full of bliss but incoherent. In their search for a substantive spirituality, they are often encouraged in this New Age to "pick what works" for them. The result can be a confusing mishmash of legitimate experience and hokum that they then try to synthesize into a workable philosophy and worldview. Such synthesis of disparate elements is not always possible—or even desirable.

The fundamental problem with this shotgun approach to enhancing awareness is that the seeker is rarely guided through it in a sequential way. Formal disciplines all have a "program" that one can work one's way through. At each step along the way, a teacher says, "Here, right here, is the state of awareness we are looking at. See it, feel it, become anchored in it, and then we shall move on." The idea is that in a formalized program, honed to perfection over the course of generations, the student works her way slowly up to the causal, and ultimate freedom, becoming anchored in each state and understanding it fully on the way up. Once in the causal, the small self drops away, and the student can re-inhabit the world at will, donning whatever mask or state she desires, because she understands through experience what it means to be that thing. She has already worked her way through it once.

Without having the benefit of a formal program, these things can be learned haphazardly and out of sequence. Seekers, improperly prepared, don't become anchored in one state before they are catapulted into another, so they end up ungrounded and confused. They may turn on the drumming to get slammed into the mid-subtle shamanic realms, then sing and dance at a kirtan to reach the high subtle, brushing the causal, then blast into Zen-based alpha-state meditation, and finally exit these and try to interact with those around them. Meanwhile, their consciousness has left a greasy smear across the cosmos, they still have the same unresolved problems they've always had, and they wonder why they can't pull their lives together.

Kabbalah for Health & Wellness provides a framework within which all of these experiences can be understood and ultimately utilized for personal wellness and evolving awareness. Mark Stavish has provided, through this book, a methodology that anchors all of the myriad states and levels of awareness in the physical. In so doing, he teaches the reader how to prepare for and enter these states in a sequence that benefits health and clarifies awareness rather than clouding and potentially injuring the psyche. Mark not only provides tools so that the reader might live life more fully, he boldly shows how to use the insight and awareness gained through these practices to purify our manifold self, preparing the way for us to interact with the world from a soul-centered rather than ego-centered frame of reference. This preparation represents a freedom that enables us to live our lives fearlessly unfettered. This is no small thing.

The reader will find that the framework Mark provides herein will not defy or contradict any doctrine they may hold dear. As with any truth-based wisdom, the practices here fit perfectly into any enlightened theology. In fact, because of its practical nature, *Kabbalah for Health & Wellness* may reinvigorate one's traditional observances.

Mark Stavish is a fine teacher and an excellent writer. He breathes new life into the dry pages of ancient wisdom and finds ways to frame the antiquated in such a way that it is instantly useful to practitioners in the twenty-first century. His words awaken the greatness of one's soul-self and remind us that although this path is an arduous one, it is traveled a bit more easily with the aid of an accomplished teacher.

May this be your experience as you make your journey to health and wellness.

Colleen Deatsman, M.A., L.P.C.
Mason, Michigan
April 2006

Introduction

Health and wellness are essential if we are to realize what modern esotericism refers to as our "True Will." To be in harmony with our innate
spiritual consciousness, and to assist others in realizing theirs, is the principal purpose of traditional esotericism. From this experience, we come
to understand the meaning of "Seek ye first the Kingdom of God and
all things shall be added unto you." Health and wellness fills our being,
giving us a more balanced emotional life, increased physical vitality, and
creativity. We become more, we express more, and we are more when in
harmony with our Inner Self. However, there seems to be a catch. While
emotional and physical health are stimulated by heightened states of
awareness, it also seems that only when we are already emotionally and
physically well can we experience these states. Clearly there is a distinct
and noticeable feedback loop between bodily health and consciousness.
And if all things are from the One and ultimately united in their source
and function, how can there not be a subtle yet powerful relationship
between these two extremes?

   Kabbalah for Health & Wellness offers a means to bridge this gap and
to utilize this relationship between "body" and "consciousness" from a
traditional Kabbalistic and Hermetic viewpoint. While energetic healing
has long been known among Kabbalists, *Kabbalah for Health & Wellness*
may very well be the first book that explains in detail the various schools
of Kabbalah, healing methods based on their principal techniques, and

their applications for both novice and experienced practitioners, integrating the most important concepts that practical Kabbalah offers. Even if you are not a Kabbalist, alchemist, or student of Hermeticism, *Kabbalah for Health & Wellness* will have something for you that will increase your knowledge of practical occultism, regardless of your tradition.

However, any esoteric practice is a process that must be undertaken with the intention to follow it through to the end and complete it. The experiences we get, as in all authentic traditions, are accumulative. If you are willing to spend a few minutes a day on what is contained in this book, you will find it time well spent, and your understanding of yourself, your health, Kabbalah, and your chosen spiritual path will improve.

Kabbalah is the core of most Western occult practices and offers its students many methods for dealing with practical issues of life, including physical, emotional, and mental health. Unfortunately, the practices more concerned with daily living have often been ignored in the rush to induce heightened states of consciousness or evoke invisible beings to visible appearance. *Kabbalah for Health & Wellness* seeks to restore this balance through a clear and simple application of traditional practices. Some of this material will be familiar to experienced students, although the application may vary from what is often taught. New students will find that Kabbalah isn't as difficult as they thought it was, and that what is often described as "Kabbalah," or "*the* tradition," is in fact just one aspect of it.

Students looking for a form of Kabbalistic or even Hermetic shamanism will find it in *Kabbalah for Health & Wellness*, as practical Kabbalah is the foundation of European folk magic, including the oldest surviving form of magic rooted in the Renaissance traditions—"pow-wow," or traditional German folk magic, common at one time among the Pennsylvania German or "Pennsylvania Dutch" communities.[1]

Modern esotericism traces itself to the ancient mystery schools, which were a continuation and outgrowth of earlier shamanic or folk magical practices. Esotericism—alchemy in particular—has always been associated

---

1 For information on German folk magic, or pow-wow, see: Karl Herr, *Hex and Spellwork: The Magical Practices of the Pennsylvania Dutch* (York Beach, ME: Weiser Books, 2002), and Mark Stavish, "Pow-Wow, Psalms, and German Magical Folklore," *Mezlim* (August 1994).

with the healing arts, with Paracelsus being the most famous physician of his day and the first Rosicrucian manifesto, the *Fama Fraternitatis,* obliging its members to heal the sick for free. However, somewhere in the sixteenth century, alchemy transformed from operative laboratory work into "transcendental" or "spiritual" alchemy. This continued until the eighteenth century, and by the nineteenth and early twentieth centuries, operative alchemy had all but disappeared and for many was seen as a purely symbolic system. Even Israel Regardie made this error in his alchemical work *The Philosopher's Stone.* He later recanted some of his statements after he came into contact with Frater Albertus and his alchemical school, the Paracelsus Research Society, in Salt Lake City, Utah.[2] Regardie eventually practiced laboratory work, even injuring his lungs in an experiment. Despite this, the transcendental idea of alchemy would—and to this day does—remain the primary theme.

The history of esotericism and its occult practices is a long and tangled one that is highlighted by the sheer degree of opposition it has experienced for nearly 1,500 years—an opposition so strong, well organized, and widespread that it is amazing anything resembling a coherent esoteric teaching survived at all.

But survive it did. Fragmented, battered, but alive, the tradition survived, demonstrating a resiliency few would have thought possible. During the Thirty Years War (1618–1648), it briefly seemed that Hermeticism might be the salvation for a war-torn Europe, uniting a continent by bridging the bloody Catholic-Protestant divide. But this did not happen, and underground again it went, surfacing occasionally in Masonic and Rosicrucian conventions of the eighteenth century but always under the watchful eye of church and state.

Only with the "Occult Revival" that occurred in France, Britain, Germany (and even the United States and Russia) in the last quarter of the nineteenth century did alchemy, Kabbalah, and astrology—the cornerstones of the Hermetic tradition—make themselves public without widespread fear of persecution.

---

2 The Paracelsus Research Society closed its doors in the mid 1980s, although several of Frater Albertus's students continue to teach practical laboratory alchemy.

Since Israel Regardie's publishing of the teachings of the Hermetic Order of the Golden Dawn in 1940, Kabbalah has slowly regained its foothold as the essential core of many, if not all, of the prominent occult practices in Western esotericism. Many decades have passed since Regardie made these critical techniques accessible to everyone seeking to realize his or her True Will. However, along with this great undertaking of keeping the Golden Dawn teachings alive, there has been a distinct bias in modern esotericism toward them, while ignoring more closely kept practices.

For many students unfamiliar with other teachings, the practices and methods of the Golden Dawn are not seen as one aspect of the Western Esoteric *Traditions*, but instead as *the* Western Esoteric Tradition. This fault is by no means Regardie's or the Golden Dawn's but instead points to the success of the teachings presented by both.

Among the missing pieces is a clear and practical application of Kabbalah, devoid of extensive ritualistic practices—Kabbalah for daily concerns, principally health and well-being.

It is important to note that *Hermeticism* is the umbrella term for the Western Esoteric Traditions as they have developed since the Renaissance. Dating back to the early Christian era, Hermeticism finds its philosophical roots in the ancient Egyptian cults. This later synthesis of Egyptian, Christian, Jewish, Gnostic, and Platonic thought with the technical applications of magic (mainly Kabbalistic), plant (spagyrics) and mineral alchemy, and astrology gave rise to what we now call Hermeticism.

The Institute for Hermetic Studies seeks to make available to students of esotericism clear, concise, and practical information on the theory and practice of Hermeticism while still remaining true to traditional ethics—and without any need for secrecy or false pretense to "protect the secrets from the profane." The secrets do not need protecting, for they are self-protected. As any student quickly discovers, if one does the work, as outlined in this or similar books, the process will unfold. If the work is not done, then no amount of reading or attempts at shortcuts will do it for anyone. Despite this, there is a danger that practical texts like this will be taken out of context. For this reason, while this book presents a great deal of information to you on the practical aspects of Kabbalah, it is critical that students realize that this is just one small part of the overall Kabbalistic traditions.

The Hermetica Healing Arts Program offered by the Institute for Hermetic Studies is an attempt to present the entire corpus of Hermetic theory and practice in a format reflecting the current needs and concerns of society. *Kabbalah for Health & Wellness* represents a small part of the total materials available to students of Hermeticism in general and Kabbalah in particular. We strongly encourage our readers to study the information in *Kabbalah for Health & Wellness* carefully and to apply it diligently in relation to their esoteric or healing-art studies.

Ora et Labora!

Mark Stavish
Director of Studies
Institute for Hermetic Studies
Wyoming, Pennsylvania
12 June 2005

How to Use This Book

Kabbalah for Health & Wellness is an introductory text on Kabbalah for students of the healing arts. Like any text on experiential mysticism or consciousness studies, *Kabbalah for Health & Wellness* contains explicit, detailed, and practical exercises that are simple to perform, transforming ideas into experiences. While it is possible to achieve results from each of the techniques presented independent of the others, it is neither desirable nor suggested that such an approach be undertaken. Each of the techniques presented in *Kabbalah for Health & Wellness* builds on the ones preceding it.

The Rituals and Practices in This Book

For too long, Kabbalah and the Hermetic traditions have been top-heavy with extensive and baroque rituals under the false guise that complexity was the same as meaning and that the effectiveness of a ritual could be measured in proportion to how long it took to perform it or the number of props needed. An argument can be made for the exact opposite: that difficult rituals are simply the constructs of insecure minds seeking assurances in a profusion of symbols to compensate for their lack of confidence. All of the exercises, rituals, practices, and techniques presented in *Kabbalah for Health & Wellness* can be performed by anyone after one or two readings of the steps involved. Their effectiveness is based on traditional symbols, key ideas, and regular practice by students, not complex thought forms, egregores, or a multitude of devices designed to build confidence in students while also developing dependency.

The premise of *Kabbalah for Health & Wellness* is to be the first book on Kabbalah that is actually *user-friendly*. Fifteen minutes a day is all that is required to turn the information it contains from theory into personal knowledge, power, and experience.

Start with each technique as it is presented. Perform it for the period suggested, which is often fifteen minutes a day for one or two weeks. Then move on to the next exercise. It is unimportant that you feel as if you have had any "success" in each exercise. Simply continue your way through. The reasons for this are simple: Each person responds differently to psycho-spiritual work, particularly if it is in a new area for them. Many of the practices given here will cover the same ideas but from different perspectives. Thus, each person may respond more strongly to one practice than to another. It is impossible to tell which that will be without first having performed them all. Think of it as a kind of Kabbalistic buffet, where you get to taste all of the offerings before going back for more of your favorite food. Another reason for performing all of the exercises included is that many of them build on one another. While it is still possible to have success if some exercises are skipped, it is also true that greater success and satisfaction will come from having performed all of them, thereby experiencing the intimate relationships discussed in the text.

Students new to Western esotericism or who have struggled with other texts in the past will notice that *Kabbalah for Health & Wellness* is written as nontechnically as possible. The book is based on two basic assumptions:

- Western esotericism can be discussed in a clear, simple, and straightforward manner and still retain its validity and authenticity.
- For any esoteric tradition to have meaning, it must be accessible, understandable, and practical.

As a result, *Kabbalah for Health & Wellness* stands out as being an ideal text for new and experienced students of spirituality for the following reasons:

- It places a great deal of emphasis on the actual performance of the exercises, thereby creating an experiential context for learning.

- All of the text is written in *English first*, with secondary references to the Hebrew, Latin, or Greek terms. This makes it easier to memorize and absorb the terms and technical information, and minimizes the need to constantly look up definitions. This is a major step forward in the process used to teach contemporary esotericism.

- Many of the techniques presented are often considered very advanced but are presented in *Kabbalah for Health & Wellness* in a manner that makes them easy to learn and apply. Regular use and practice will allow students to quickly identify their strong points as well as the exercises that need their additional attention for an even and balanced development of healing skill and technique.

- It features clear identification and use of the practical material presented, using the following definitions: *Exercises*—methods designed to strengthen specific mental or psychic functions or to reinforce a theoretical point; *Techniques*—methods that have a specific use and function alone or in combination; *Practices*—specific techniques designed to enhance spiritual awakening and, thereby, healing potential; *Core Practices*—practices that form part of a student's daily and weekly practice schedule.

Ideally, *Kabbalah for Health & Wellness* would be used in connection with a regular study group or as part of the Hermetica Healing Arts courses offered by the Institute for Hermetic Studies. However, personal instruction is not always possible, nor is it necessary if students carry out the simple and easy-to-follow instructions and give themselves sufficient time to intellectually and psychically assimilate the ideas presented. Nothing can speed up this process; only constant, steady, and heartfelt practice can move it along.

It is important to state that modern esotericism is radically different from its predecessors. It is practiced, for the most part, out of its cultural context with information transmitted in manners undreamed of by earlier students and adepts. The closely guarded and tightly knit relationship between students and teacher-initiator no longer exists. This has led many to believe that a teacher is not necessary, as they have the "Inner Master" to guide them. This is true only insofar as all students have the personal discipline, self-reflection, and honesty to listen to the words of their Inner Master. Until that time, an "outer teacher" will be needed. It is hoped that this book will act in some fashion as that outer teacher.

If at this point you may be thinking that there is an easier way, let us state firmly and unequivocally that there is not. If psychic development, alchemical transformation, or cosmic consciousness were easy, the world would be a paradise, and Illumination a common experience. The Path of Becoming is the Great Work. It is the single greatest challenge and undertaking anyone can pursue. Its rewards come daily in small, mostly unnoticed ways, all culminating in that moment when the Great Awakening will occur. If you wish to take the quick and easy road, then stop looking, for none exists except the road of sorrow and disappointment. Magic, alchemy, and spiritual healing are not for the lazy but for the brave. When we say that you can progress by dedicating as little as fifteen minutes a day, this requires regularity and consistency. At this rate, you will experience results confirming your Path in about eighteen to twenty-four months. In general, the material contained in *Kabbalah for Health & Wellness* will take you about three years to complete. Within that time, you will see, feel, and integrate into your body and psyche many changes. While it seems that this is all up to you, and you know not what you are doing, where you are going, or what to expect, know that there are invisible aids helping you all along—friends, strangers, books like this—that will come to you in times of need, until you are able to listen to the voice of the Inner Master and need to read no more.

No matter what, remember this: by the very fact that you call upon God, the archangels, the invisible ones of Creation, they respond and are present with you. They are always there, and in our petition, we become aware of them.

Since many have chosen to read and practice *Kabbalah for Health &
Wellness* with the intention to heal others, now is a good time to point
out that while integrating Kabbalah into a healing practice, you should
view the ability to heal more as a side effect of your understanding of
Kabbalah rather than an end in itself. That is, you should not study Kabbalah with the point of view that it is another "technology" or "method"
for strictly utilitarian means. Kabbalah is to be studied as a path to Illumination, and as a result of that Illumination, certain gifts are bestowed along
the way. *Kabbalah for Health & Wellness* points out what some of these gifts
are and how they can be better developed and integrated, not as ends in
and of themselves. This being said, it is important to try to assist people
when the opportunity presents itself. It is amazing how in times of crises
and emergency we can release a tremendous amount of healing ability
that otherwise seemed unavailable to us. Thus, by studying *Kabbalah for
Health & Wellness*, you will have certain channels and tools ready-made
should you encounter those emergencies; even small results from when
you try to assist others increase your self-confidence in your chosen Path
and, as a result, make future success more likely. The ability to heal—or
any gift—is a confirmation of your work, nothing more and nothing less.

Establishing a Program

1. Daily practice is essential. Establish a regular daily schedule for fifteen
   minutes a day. The more time you spend on the techniques described
   in *Kabbalah for Health & Wellness*, the more proficient you will become in them, the easier Kabbalah will be for you to apply, and the
   more enjoyable it will be. If you have the opportunity to spend a few
   minutes during the day working on a particular visualization or meditation in addition to your regular program, all the better. In fact, it is
   better to have three or four short sessions a day for ten or fifteen minutes than to try to cram everything into one long session. The brain
   and the stomach like their food in small, digestible doses several times
   a day rather than in one sitting. Psychological and spiritual exercises
   also require time for their seeds to reach fruition. This is often measured in astrological cycles, be they lunar (a month) or solar (a year),

and for this reason specific directions advise how long to practice an exercise.

2. Keep a notebook of your experiences. This is important for self-review and in understanding your dream life and the activation of symbols within your psyche.

3. If possible, set aside a special place just for this work. If that is not possible, use a regular opening and closing ritual (such as the one that will be given) to set the proper atmosphere for the work to be performed.

4. Be regular in your time of practice as well. By creating healthy habits of time and place, we make our study period something we look forward to and enjoy.

5. "Make haste slowly." Spend the proper amount of time on each exercise, move on to the next, and complete each phase of practice in order with a calm, relaxed confidence that everything is working inside you just as it should. You will surprise yourself at the power and ability you possess. It is there when you need it, even if you are not always conscious of it.

6. Take notes as you read. Write down the key ideas as they are presented so that you are better able to remember and apply them. To assist in this, words in Hebrew, Latin, Greek, or any language other than English follow their modern equivalent in parentheses. Get the core ideas down first; then go back and learn the vocabulary.

7. *Kabbalah for Health & Wellness* contains a glossary of many of the specialized words used in the text. To make reading and using this book easier, it was decided to limit the amount of non-English words used. It is important that you learn these words, as other texts are often not as user-friendly. Also, these words are the technical language of Kabbalah.

8. Finally, study with a friend or two if possible. The power of collective work to spark individual insights and transformations is well documented. The Gospels say it simply: "Where two or more are gathered together in my Name, I will be in the midst of them." Two or three students working regularly have often produced marvelous results and have historically been the basis for some of the most important esoteric (as well as exoteric) organizations in history.

Chapter 1

What Is Energetic Healing?

Energetic healing is a traditional method of using the physical and psychic energies of the body to assist in the healing process. While primarily directed at achieving various degrees of physical wellness and health, energetic healing recognizes the importance of emotional and mental wellness in the healing process. In many ways, energetic healing affects the physical body by first creating healthy changes in the mind.

While many systems of energetic healing exist and are prominent in India, China, and across the East, it is generally thought that Europe and America had "outgrown" these ideas. This idea has become so embedded in the popular mindset that many people do not even realize that there have always been several distinct and vibrant forms of esotericism in European and American culture. Among these practices has been the use of energetic healing, including prayer, meditation, visualization, and ritual. Herbal and metallic products are also used and form the basis of modern concepts of alchemy, herbalism, spagyrics (plant alchemy), and even homeopathy.

7

However, it is the use of the mind in creating and maintaining health and wellness that has always been the most common practice. This is in part due to the ability to utilize mind-based techniques almost anywhere, in many instances, by anyone.

It is important to recognize that esoteric systems are in fact a mirror, product, and guide for the cultures in which they exist. Symbols give meaning to daily experiences, and those experiences take place in a distinct geographical environment. It is from those experiences that symbols are created and used to give meaning to events. As these symbols and their meanings grow, esoteric systems are progressively created. When a system is divorced from its geographic context and its culture of origin, it either becomes heavily watered down or simply archaic and ineffective. At worst, it becomes a novelty for dilettantism or completely meaningless, having no cultural touchstones to orient the practitioner.

As such, it is important to recognize that for the last thousand years Hermeticism has been the main thrust of the various esoteric systems of the West. Hermeticism has been both the seed and the fruit of millennia of spiritual research and practices across the Mediterranean basin, and during the Renaissance it acted as a focal point for the progress of Western civilization.

Hermeticism was so successful in its opening up of the collective European mind that it essentially put itself out of business through its natural extension in the eighteenth and nineteenth centuries with the Age of Reason and the Industrial Revolution. The experiential model that is the basis for all occult practices is expressed daily through the "scientific model." Modern science is in many ways the distorted expression of ancient esoteric doctrines and occult practices, of which energetic healing was a daily experience.

This is important, for as healing tells us, nothing happens in a vacuum. Any single idea taken to an extreme creates imbalance, be it in individuals or in societies. This is the first and most important point in energetic healing:

All things in moderation.

To dismiss the important advantages of modern medicine to the physical sciences is as dangerous an extreme as to embrace only the things we can touch with the senses. If everything comes from "the One," then everything is an expression of its energy and intelligence. Physical "things" can be just as spiritual as the highest archangel, and spiritual ideals can be turned into little more than self-aggrandizing materials in the wrong hands. We need to be moderate and temperate in all of our views and actions if we are to be healthy and spiritually whole.

This leads us to our second point:

Use material medicines when needed, and recognize their value and importance as a very real and concrete expression of spiritual principles.

The ancients expressed this in what is called the Hermetic axiom, commonly stated as, "As above, so below."

A more accurate translation in full reads: "That which is above comes from that which is below. That which is below comes from that which is above . . . from the One Thing."

The "One Thing" is the energy of creation, its total intelligence, love, and creative ability. All things exist because of the One Thing, and everything exists within it and as an expression of it. On an absolute level, it is the Void; on a practical level, it is the Prima Materia ("First Matter") of the alchemists that is used in all operations and described as being "common and found everywhere."

Seven Principles of Energetic Healing

1. The health of the body reflects our consciousness.

2. All comes from the One Thing: "As above, so below."

3. All things exist as an adaptation or modification of the original seed, the One Thing. This is the Chaos or Hyle of alchemy and the Nothingness (Ain Soph Aur) of Kabbalah.

4. We assist Nature. The physical world has some energy and a great deal of matter, but very little consciousness. As participants in the process, we add consciousness to assist in directing the energy-matter to the desired expression. We are coworkers with Nature.

5. Universal justice, or *karma*, must be properly understood for healing to take place.

6. When faced with a life-threatening condition, a compelling reason to live—beyond simply being afraid to die—must be the motivator.

7. It is the duty of each to prepare in life for death, so that when it comes, we may transition more easily to the invisible worlds.

Three Major Sources of Energetic Healing in Western Esotericism

1. *Alchemy*—understanding the relation of energy and consciousness to matter. This is most easily understood in, but not limited to, modern schools of homeopathy, herbalism, and spagyrics.

2. *Kabbalah*—understanding the relation of symbols to consciousness and matter. This is most easily understood in, but not limited to, modern schools of transpersonal psychology, psychosynthesis, and even medical hypnosis. Moreover, schools of practical occultism, particularly those derived from the Hermetic Order of the Golden Dawn, Martinism, and Rosicrucianism, utilize Kabbalah-based symbols in ritual formats for healing, manipulation of material events, and the expansion of consciousness into the spiritual realms.

3. *Astrology*—understanding the relation of cycles to consciousness and matter. This is most easily understood in terms of, but is not limited to, seasonal changes and biorhythms, as well as specialized areas of medical and horary astrology.

Combined, these form the primary disciplines of the Hermetic arts and sciences, with astrology telling us who we are, Kabbalah telling us where we are going, and alchemy providing us the method of realization.

In this book, the focus is healing from the viewpoint of energy and symbolism, but to make it concrete we will weave in some of the more practical areas of alchemy and astrology that cross over with Kabbalah.

The school of Kabbalah we are discussing falls under the domain of the Hermetic Kabbalah, because it most closely resembles the Kabbalistic doctrines and practices that came out of the Renaissance and were resurrected in force during the nineteenth and twentieth centuries' Occult

Revival period. This merging of the two schools resulted in a new synthesis—a synthesis that was essential given the politics of the time. Hermeticism brought a sense of classical dignity to Kabbalistic studies, which elevated them out of being a purely Jewish subject as well as made Kabbalah more "philosophical" and less "religious" in appearance. In turn, Kabbalah brought to Hermeticism a Biblical basis, even if a non-Jewish one, as well as practical methods of working that were still understood, respected, and even feared in a hostile, anti-Jewish Catholic Europe. Thus, it is important to have an understanding of both traditional Hermetic and Kabbalistic philosophy if we are to put Kabbalah into practice.

Hermetic Philosophy

Hermeticism is the study of the body of Greek texts appearing in Alexandria, Egypt, between the first and third centuries AD and attributed to Hermes Trismegistos, as well as variations of these writings, adaptations of them, and commentaries on them up to and including the current era. These commentaries include Alexandrian as well as neo-Alexandrian traditions. The traditions are comprised of core texts, commentaries on these texts, and specific practices designed to integrate the ideas into the practitioner's life. It is clear from the texts that communities were formed in which members held communal meals, exchanged the kiss of peace, and performed initiations into the sacred mysteries. These traditions include a variety of Gnostic, Christian, Rosicrucian, and even Masonic writing groups from the first century AD and across the Renaissance, into and including orders and societies rising out of several modern and contemporary occult revivals.

Named after their attributed author, Hermes Trismegistos, or "Hermes the Thrice Great," these writings are collectively called the "Hermetica." This body of texts is small, and it has been translated several times in recent decades. Its main themes are the creation of the material world and the soul's journey, ascent, and regeneration as it progresses through the celestial spheres.

It is important to note that the Hermetic texts were composed in different time periods by different authors from different traditions. The influence of Egyptian, Greek, Jewish, and Gnostic thought is clearly present. What makes this unique is that despite these diverse influences, Hermeticism manages to synthesize the ideas presented and create a distinct school of thought that goes beyond each of them individually. Names and ideas of one tradition are seamlessly intermingled and interpreted according to the ideas of another.

Alexandrian Hermeticism and modern Hermetic practices share four key points, including a synthetic philosophy that, while utilizing the mythology of "fall and regeneration," avoids the pitfalls of dualism and emphasizes concrete and commonsense approaches to solving mundane as well as cosmological issues.[1] Hermeticism encourages and embraces the notion of humanity and the Divine existing harmoniously in and through the world. It is an exceedingly optimistic philosophy and, in this regard, very different from certain strains of Gnosticism, or even Vedantic studies, which see the world at best as an essential evil for the soul's growth and at worst as a prison house and punishment for some distant and long-forgotten transgression.

The eclectic nature of Hermeticism comes from its fundamental premise that the desire for knowledge can be satisfied by consulting a variety of sources that find their roots in the *philosophia perennis*, or "perennial philosophy." It is synthetic in that these diverse ideas are not only tolerated, but unified into a seamless whole.

Nous means "mind," and Hermes is informed by Nous (his Higher Self) to meditate on the nature of the universe being reflected in his own being, to extract the divine powers of Nature and unite them with the powers of his soul. The universe is a text to be read—"The Book of Nature"—and through our divine intellect, we are able to unite with it and understand it.

The physical world is a good place, and it is essential to the unfolding of human consciousness. Hermeticism reaches the abstract through the concrete. The universe is met in the mineral salts of an herbal (spagyric) tincture; the psychic centers or "stars" are experienced through the influ-

---

1 Antoine Faivre, "Hermeticism," in *The Encyclopedia of Religion*, ed. Mircea Eliade, 16 vols. (New York: Macmillan, 1996), 293–302.

ence of the planets on one's personal horoscope.[2] Hermeticism is very specific, personal, and experiential, and yet it continually transcends the limits of material life. This natural magic gives rise to natural philosophy, and the Divine is seen incarnate everywhere and in everyone.

The Emerald Tablet of Hermes

True, without error, certain and most true;

That which is above is as that which is below, and that which is below is as that which is above, for performing the miracle of the One Thing (or One Substance); and as all things were from one, by the mediation of one, so all things arose from this one thing by adaptation; the father of it is the Sun; the mother of it is the Moon; the wind carries it in its belly; the nurse thereof is the Earth.

This is the father of all perfection, of consummation of the whole world.

The power of it is integral, if it be turned into earth.

Thou shalt separate the earth from the fire, the subtle from the gross, gently with much sagacity;

it ascends from the earth to heaven, and again descends to earth; and receives the strength of the superiors and of the inferiors—so thou hast the glory of the whole world;

therefore let all obscurity flee before thee.

This is the strong fortitude of all fortitudes, overcoming every subtle and penetrating every solid thing.

So the world was created.

Hence were all wonderful adaptations of which this is the manner.

Therefore am I called Thrice Great Hermes, having Three Parts of the philosophy of the whole world.

That which I have written is consummated concerning the operation of the Sun.[3]

Commentary on the Emerald Tablet of Hermes

1. *"True, without error, certain and most true"*

The author is stating that the following statements are complete, whole, and true, without exception, anywhere and anytime. It is a universal truth that is about to be given. This is also a statement of confidence that brings

---

2 Astrology in Alexandrian Hermeticism is initiatic and represents the journey of the individual as well as the collective soul on the "Path of Return" or regeneration. Since the seventeenth century, however, astrology has increasingly become little more than a form of divination divorced from spiritual practices and understanding.

3 Frater Achad, *The Egyptian Revival; or, The Ever-Coming Son in the Light of the Tarot* (York Beach, ME: Weiser, 1974), chapter 8. Also available online at http://www.hermetic.com/browe-archive/achad/egyptian/egypt1.htm.

the mind of readers or listeners to a sense of assuredness about what they are about to hear. Without this confidence as a foundation, no practical application can succeed.

2. *"That which is above is as that which is below, and that which is below is as that which is above, for performing the miracle of the One Thing"*

This is the most critical axiom of Hermeticism. All schools of classical esotericism, as well as those derived from them, make this the central philosophical idea, with all practical applications being based on it.

The inner and outer worlds are perfect mirrors of one another. To understand one gives understanding in the other. To act in one is to act in the other. This is why actions in dreams or visualized states can materialize and why rituals in the material world can affect the inner life. This essential unity is the One Thing, and its "miracle" is the evolution of consciousness, of life.

3. *". . . and as all things were from one, by the mediation of the one, so all things arose from this one thing by adaptation; the father of it is the Sun; the mother of it is the Moon; the wind carries it in its belly; the nurse thereof is the Earth."*

Here again, the Oneness of everything is affirmed. Differences are but adaptations or selected expressions of the nature of Oneness. Its active or generating part is the Sun, and its passive or form-giving part is the Moon. The wind, or air, carries this life energy, this essential consciousness, deep within itself, and through material life it is nurtured and grows.

4. *"This is the father of all perfection, of consummation of the whole world."*

This foundational unity is the source of all perfection, and through it, the material world is brought to a higher level of expression, mirroring the invisible.

5. *"The power of it is integral, if it be turned into earth."*

Without this unity, nothing can be achieved, and when the subtle becomes dense, or material, it contains within itself the seeds of unity despite the image of separation.

6. *"Thou shalt separate the earth from the fire, the subtle from the gross, gently with much sagacity; it ascends from the earth to heaven, and again descends to earth; and*

receives the strength of the superiors and of the inferiors—so thou hast the glory of the whole world; therefore let all obscurity flee before thee."

In the creation of physical life, energy went from being very subtle to very dense. Matter is concentrated energy. It is in fact solidified light, or, as the ancients would have called it, fire. This fire is the subtle energy, and the earth is its dense counterpart, or offspring. In matter, or earth, there is a great deal of potential energy stored or compressed that can be released and directed according to occult operations. This energy also has the potential to gain in strength through movement, and so it is "ascending and descending" between the extremes of energy and matter. From this we are given an additional Hermetic-alchemical axiom: *"solve et coagula,"* or "dissolve and recombine." Through constant dissolving and recombining in the energy-matter relationship, our understanding of how these two poles interact is strengthened as well as purified. Thus, ignorance of life, "all obscurity," is removed.

7. *"This is the strong fortitude of all fortitudes, overcoming every subtle and penetrating every solid thing."*

Through the process of "solve et coagula," all obstacles are overcome and every subtle or solid thing (philosophical point, astral impulse, or material object) can be understood and put to service.

8. *"So the world was created. Hence were all wonderful adaptations of which this is the manner."*

This simple process is the process whereby creation took place, and everything is a modification of its basic principles.

9. *"Therefore am I called Thrice Great Hermes, having Three Parts of the philosophy of the whole world. That which I have written is consummated concerning the operation of the Sun."*

"Thrice Great," because Hermes has knowledge that can allow him to act in all three worlds of ancient cosmology: infernal, natural, and celestial. It is consummated—or achieved, perfected, and carried out—through this simple process. The operation of the sun, the source of energy and matter in our solar system, is brought to perfection by the adept or "Philosopher" who understands and uses this knowledge.

In *The Great Monochord*, Robert Fludd, the last great Renaissance Magi, wrote:

> "The monad (one thing) generates a monad and reflects its ardour in itself. The One is all things and all things are the One. GOD is all that there is; from him all things proceed and to him all things must return. The Infinite dimensions of the Tetragrammaton: in and between all things."[4]

Renaissance and the Hermetic Ideal

During the Renaissance, Guidorno Bruno, one of the most famous of the Italian magi, was martyred in the name of science. He was burned at the stake in 1500 for his cosmological propositions, an action the Roman Catholic Church apologized for in 2000. Bruno's ideal "Renaissance man" (or woman) was not just well educated in the arts, sciences, and philosophies, but also put them into practice in their most perfect synthetic expression—Hermeticism. The practicing Hermeticist was an alchemist, Kabbalist, astrologist, and, as such, a magus. For Bruno, however, this meant that the magus was first a physician and healed the physical and psychological wounds of the individual. The magus was also a prophet, in line with the prophets of the Old Testament; that is, they spoke out to warn the community of possible problems and hardships if continued courses of action were taken and, in doing so, helped heal the community and keep it in harmony with divine laws. Finally, he or she was a true magus, or master of the occult arts, and co-creator with the Divine. In modern esoteric terms, we might see this as the shaman, the priest/priestess, and the magus/magician. Some insight into the relationship of these three roles can be found in the major arcana using the following table:

Bruno	Modern	Tarot Card	Alternate
Physician	Shaman	Emperor	Empress
Prophet	Priest	Hierophant	Priestess
Magus	Magus	Magician	The World

---

4 Joscelyn Godwin, *Robert Fludd: Hermetic Philosopher and Surveyor of Two Worlds* (Boston: Phanes Press, 2005), 52.

The Focus of *Kabbalah for Health & Wellness*

Based on the preceding introduction, *Kabbalah for Health & Wellness* will demonstrate how to take the fundamental ideas presented in traditional Kabbalah and its Hermetic cousin and apply them in practical ways. These practices will demonstrate the importance of the five key steps in both healing and spiritual awakening or Illumination: (1) purification, (2) imprinting, (3) activating, (4) transmuting, and (5) direct experience.

Purification—Preparing the mind and body for new experiences and energy by first cleaning out the old, worn-out, and defective energies that are creating emotional, mental, or physical illness.

Imprinting—Consciously imprinting new ideas, images, symbols, sounds, and other useful devices into the etheric and psychic bodies so that the desired states of health and consciousness can be facilitated.

Activating—Consciously, methodically, and confidently turning on the new "imprints" so that they may work toward the desired end. This along with imprinting is critical to any genuine esoteric initiation.

Transmuting—Working directly with destructive or negative energies and using them in a new context or modifying them so that they are no longer an obstacle in your spiritual path or that of another. This phase does not "purify" negative energies by getting rid of them and replacing them with new energy, but instead works directly with them and literally changes them into something more desirable.

Direct Experience—This phase is a synthesis of the previous phases and involves direct experiences of wellness either in body or consciousness without the intermediary steps of either purification or transmutation. It also involves experiencing the new states as they arise—or after consciously creating them—and simply resting or sitting in the experience while holding it as long as possible.

What Are Illness and Health?

In Western esotericism, illness is seen as natural. It occurs and is part of life. While it demonstrates an area of imbalance in our inner or psychic being manifesting in our physical bodies, it is nonetheless part of human life. Illness reminds us of the fleeting nature of our lives and of the need to achieve or accomplish whatever it is that we desire to do. It is a wake-up call to the soul to get moving. The same is true with death. Death cannot be avoided. Even if immortality is possible with alchemical products, it is an immortality of consciousness that is produced, not that of the body. The Elixir of Life is a byproduct of the Philosopher's Stone, thereby allowing the alchemist to finish his or her work. Long life was enjoyed and seen as a tool for the perfection of Being, rather than an end in itself. The same is true in Chinese, Indian, Tibetan, and other Eastern traditions, where "long life" practices are undertaken for oneself or one's teacher in order to attain perfect enlightenment. Health and life are but vehicles we use to achieve and accomplish things in life. This is why having a reason to live gives us the power to live, rather than simply the desire to continue out of fear of death.

The Importance of Imperturbability

Positive indifference is key to living a happy and healthy life. By being undisturbed by life's experiences, be they good or bad, we develop a sense of positive indifference. By that we mean that we understand the things that we can change and we act accordingly; we also understand that getting upset about what we cannot change only makes situations worse and drags us down in useless suffering.

The Greek philosophy of Stoicism is key to this approach, and it is also the cornerstone of Buddhist practices. If we seek to avoid destructive situations, we must avoid destructive habits. Habits are unconscious responses to situations and are built up over time. They become so ingrained that, like a computer program, we automatically respond in a predictable manner. This is the true meaning of karma: habitual thought streams, energized by emotions, that act as causes for new experiences, connected to the type and quality of emotions and thoughts that created them.

If we seek to avoid karma, we must simply not respond to situations in a powerful and emotional manner—particularly not with negative and destructive emotions.

We must learn to be indifferent to life's circumstances and proceed with our chosen goal, practice, or activity regardless. This does not mean that we do not enjoy the positive things of life, only that we accept that they are temporary and that all things change. It is the desire to calcify and make permanent an experience that adds to our suffering and prevents us from learning the true meaning of life.

If you are working with people who have requested spiritual assistance with their healing processes, it is important that you discuss this with them and help them understand their true motivations for seeking health. Without proper intention or right motivation, any efforts at spiritual healing will be compromised. The same holds true with any efforts we make when seeking to make progress on the Path.

Each of us is filled with "likes" and "dislikes," which are an extension and continuation of our ignorance. If we seek Illumination, or to be filled with light, we must be open to experiences and find their meaning, rather than run to or from them because of unconscious reactions. Imperturbability is based on the premise that nothing is permanent, nor as it seems, and that our inner conviction toward the Truth is all that is important. This allows us to be open to each experience and to extract its essence.

Likes and dislikes are always preceded by "I." We say, "I like this" or "I don't like that." This is the ego talking. While it may be unrealistic at this point for many people to remain completely unmoved emotionally or mentally if forced to eat cow dung, it is important that the foundational ideal of imperturbability and positive indifference always be a part of our daily practice. This cannot be understated; it is the key to all progress.

Rudyard Kipling, author and Freemason, wrote a poem based on the following story, which is found in the Talmud:

Solomon and the Ring of Power

One day, Solomon decided to humble Benaiah ben Yehoyada, his most trusted minister. He said to him, "Benaiah, there is a certain ring that I want you to bring to me. I wish to wear it for Sukkot, which gives you six months to find it."

"If it exists anywhere on earth, your majesty," replied Benaiah, "I will find it and bring it to you, but what makes the ring so special?"

"It has magic powers," answered the king. "If a happy man looks at it, he becomes sad, and if a sad man looks at it, he becomes happy." Solomon knew that no such ring existed in the world, but he wished to give his minister a little taste of humility.

Spring passed and then summer, and still Benaiah had no idea where he could find the ring. On the night before Sukkot, he decided to take a walk in one of the poorest quarters of Jerusalem. He passed by a merchant who had begun to set out the day's wares on a shabby carpet. "Have you by any chance heard of a magic ring that makes the happy wearer forget his joy and the broken-hearted wearer forget his sorrows?" asked Benaiah.

He watched the grandfather take a plain gold ring from his carpet and engrave something on it. When Benaiah read the words on the ring, his face broke out in a wide smile. That night, the entire city welcomed in the holiday of Sukkot with great festivity. "Well, my friend," said Solomon, "have you found what I sent you after?" All the ministers laughed, and Solomon himself smiled.

To everyone's surprise, Benaiah held up a small gold ring and declared, "Here it is, your majesty!" As soon as Solomon read the inscription, the smile vanished from his face. The jeweler had written three Hebrew letters on the gold band: "Gimel, Zayin, Yod," which began the words "Gam zeh ya'avor"—"This too shall pass."

At that moment, Solomon realized that all his wisdom and fabulous wealth and tremendous power were but fleeting things, for one day he would be nothing but dust.

Without positive indifference, or imperturbability and its strengthening, no real progress can be made in life; otherwise, what is experienced will be suffering and sorrow. What we enjoy and what brings us pain are all temporary. Wisdom, peace, and lasting happiness—the fruits of genuine health and well-being—can only be found in the mature seed of imperturbability.

Rudyard Kipling's poem *If* summarizes the essential character traits needed to undertake the spiritual path. Read it daily and meditate on its lessons. Leave a copy with those whom you may be assisting through spiritual healing practices so that they may have the opportunity to use it as a sort of character review and turn their healing practice into a genuine inner healing.

If you can keep your head when all about you
Are losing theirs and blaming it on you,
If you can trust yourself when all men doubt you
But make allowance for their doubting too,
If you can wait and not be tired by waiting,
Or being lied about, don't deal in lies,
Or being hated, don't give way to hating,
And yet don't look too good, nor talk too wise:

If you can dream—and not make dreams your master,
If you can think—and not make thoughts your aim;
If you can meet with Triumph and Disaster
And treat those two impostors just the same;
If you can bear to hear the truth you've spoken
Twisted by knaves to make a trap for fools,
Or watch the things you gave your life to, broken,
And stoop and build 'em up with worn-out tools:

If you can make one heap of all your winnings
And risk it all on one turn of pitch-and-toss,
And lose, and start again at your beginnings
And never breathe a word about your loss;
If you can force your heart and nerve and sinew
To serve your turn long after they are gone,
And so hold on when there is nothing in you
Except the Will which says to them: "Hold on!"

If you can talk with crowds and keep your virtue,
Or walk with kings—nor lose the common touch,
If neither foes nor loving friends can hurt you;
If all men count with you, but none too much,
If you can fill the unforgiving minute
With sixty seconds' worth of distance run,
Yours is the Earth and everything that's in it,
And—which is more—you'll be a Man, my son!

Purification Practices

Before beginning any period of meditation, prayer, or spiritual attunement, it is critical that we first recognize our errors and shortcomings in order to overcome them. If we mistakenly think that we can engage in spiritual practices for physical healing and not address the underlying cause within our psyche, we are destined to fail. Traditionally, reflection on one's thoughts, words, and deeds would lead to a sincere confession of sins (errors), as well as the heartfelt desire to avoid these in the future and replace them with positive thoughts, words, and acts.

While some modern practitioners may find this "too religious," it is important to remember that we cannot divorce mysticism from daily religious duties that are fundamentally moral and ethical in nature. It is only since the end of World War II that schools of esotericism have sprung up that suggest the universe is somehow "neutral" and that magic is a technology that can be used like a computer, where one punches a button and the program runs. If this were so, all would-be magicians would be wealthy, immortal, and forever happy. The training required to be proficient in esotericism takes months and years to perfect—and then we are talking about technical proficiency, not the total purification of consciousness required to be free from suffering, illness, and death as we know them.

While this kind of hard and serious assessment may be too much for some people, or while they honestly may not be in conscious recognition of an error, they can still engage in general purification practices either as a stand-alone practice or in conjunction with other work.

Students familiar with basic visualization methods may feel free to undertake the following purification practice. Newer students may simply want to read through it and familiarize themselves with the basic ideas presented and substitute an act of verbal contrition for the visualization part. This is simply done by openly and honestly confessing our errors, mistakes, and ignorance to our Inner Self as if we were talking to a close friend, and asking that our spiritual friend, our Inner Self, remove these obstacles and fill us with the energies of light, life, and love to continue on our journey toward Illumination. This form of verbal confession, especially when spoken out loud, is particularly powerful. It both invokes the secret power of the Word, which we will discuss later, and unites our aspirations with the material world. It is important that students work out the details themselves; experienced students will find combining the verbal confession with the visualization that follows to be extremely beneficial.

The following exercise is taken directly from the symbolism of the Emerald Tablet, as well as the famous alchemical symbol of the sun and the moon pouring their energies into a chalice supported by Mercury, surrounded by additional symbols, and around which is inscribed "Visitae Interia Terra, Rectificando Lapidium," translated as, "Visit the interior of the earth, and there you will make right [rectify] the Stone." Freemasonry uses similar symbolism when it refers to the "rough ashlar" and the "smooth ashlar," or rough and smooth building stones. Through our work and effort, we smooth out the roughness of our character and make ourselves worthy and talented craftsmen for building a better life.

Exercise—Simple Purification Practice

Preparation—Sit comfortably with your back straight, your feet flat on the floor, the palms of your hands flat on your thighs and close to your hips (to take stress off your shoulders and elbows), and your chin slightly tucked. Breathe deeply several times, hold your breath for as long as is comfortable, exhale slowly, and hold your breath out for as long as is comfortable. Feel yourself relax mentally, emotionally, and physically as you do this. Say the following prayer (or something similar): "Divine Mind, Source of all, assist me in this work of purification of thought, word, and deed, so that I will awaken to the innermost depths of my Being."

Explanation—This practice prepares the mind and psychic body of the practitioner for experiencing increased psychic and mystical states by decreasing the amount of psychic resistance within the mind and body of the practitioner. This focus on decreasing unconscious, internal resistance prior to additional practices makes this a purification as well as a preliminary practice.

Type of Practice—This is a preliminary practice designed to be used prior to meditation, prayer, or healing intervention. It can also be done alone in the evening or before sleep.

Method—Proceed as follows:
1. While seated, visualize the sun and moon above you. The sun is on your right, and the moon on your left. Imagine their powerful energies drawn together, as the sun brings life energy and the moon absorbs it into itself, giving form.

2. The two energies mix and project a point of energy, forming an invisible triangle that points downward into the top of your head. This energy enters into your body, filling it with brilliant, vibrant light. Imagine that all of the negative energies are pushed out of your lower openings and absorbed by the earth.

3. Imagine the fiery heat and energy of the earth (the Secret Fire) purifying the emotional, psychic, and mental refuse that you have ejected.

4. Imagine yourself filled with this brilliant and dynamic energy of the sun and the moon, radiating outward from you, and the purification, happiness, and stability that it brings. Rest in this feeling.

5. Close your meditation with a prayer of gratitude for what you have experienced and dedicate any benefits from it to your Path of Becoming and to that of others.

Incorporation into Daily Practice—This practice should take about ten to fifteen minutes at most and should be done once or twice a day for a month to get some grounded experience in the importance of purification practices in all spiritual work. Failure to undertake purification practices is tantamount to pouring fresh water into a dirty vessel. Over time, it will eventually get clean, but the process will be much more difficult than if a little soap and elbow grease had been used in the beginning. If you have a strong attraction to alchemical symbolism, you can use the Solar King and Lunar Queen in place of the sun and moon symbols.[5] More advanced purification practices are especially important when undertaking techniques involving the formation and use of the Body of Light (creation of a vehicle for conscious survival after death), astral projection, and similar advanced work.

The practice of purification can be performed by and taught to anyone who seeks to proceed on a spiritual path—more importantly, on a Hermetic, Kabbalistic, or alchemical one. It is very important, and the foundation upon which all following practices are built.

---

5 Freemasons will recognize the presence of the sun and the moon as two of the three Lesser Lights of the Lodge, with the Master, balancing and directing their energies, as the third of the Lesser Lights.

The Most Important Thing You Will Ever Read

Modern spirituality is filled with lies, half-truths, and misconceptions, all designed to part would-be seekers from their cash as well as their self-respect. Here is the sum of all truths; meditate on it and everything else will fall into its proper perspective.

1. There can be no physical healing without emotional healing first; there can be no emotional healing without first enlarging our spiritual view; there can be no spiritual growth without ethical growth first. Spirituality, healing, and ethics are all synonymous.

2. Devotion and discipline are the most important qualities for pursuing the Path—devotion to the ideal and regular practice.

3. Practice often. Remind yourself daily, even hourly if only for a moment, that all is One and that you abide in the power, wisdom, and happiness of divine tranquility. From this, feel within yourself that you can solve all problems and resolve all inconsistencies.

4. Develop the trait of positive indifference or imperturbability. Recognize all situations in life as an expression of your own Inner Self, and recognize that through them you can remove the habitual stains (karma) on your consciousness that obscure the Inner Light. See both the enjoyable and the sorrowful as expressions of the same truth.

5. Everything is in constant flux; everything changes. Neither health nor sickness, life nor death, are permanent states of being. Only consciousness is eternal.

6. Fear born of ignorance of our limitless nature is the source of all suffering, illness, and pain in human life.

7. The subconscious synthesizes our experiences to produce "order out of Chaos." To assist it, we need to pick a spiritual discipline and stick to it. Hopping from system to system looking for the magic key, or for the false ideal of some kind of multicultural eclecticism, produces only confusion and spiritual failure. Universal truths exist, but they are always presented and used in a synthetic manner in

authentic systems, not attached to each other like poorly designed additions to a home.

8. Seek to serve rather than to be served.

In the end, all esoteric practices are based on the simple truth that we become what we identify with. Through various methods, we can come to see life as the Path, and the Path as a process whereby we become the object of our heart's desire. The single greatest thing we must overcome is our own fear—the "Guardian of the Threshold."

Key Points

- Energetic healing is a traditional method of using psychic energies to bring health and wholeness to the physical and psychic bodies.

- Western esotericism and energetic-healing practices are rooted in Alexandrian and Renaissance Hermeticism.

- The Emerald Tablet of Hermes is the most important and well-known statement of Hermetic principles.

- Astrology, alchemy, and Kabbalah are the three main expressions of the Hermetic arts and sciences and are directly concerned with healing physical and psychic bodies.

- Health and wellness express themselves in having a specific reason to live, not just a fear of death.

- Imperturbability, or positive indifference, is the key to spiritual development.

- Purification practices are important, as they help us consciously address negative blocks, remove them, and replace them with positive, health-affirming energies.

Assignments for Chapter 1

1. Obtain several notebooks or a large three-ring binder divided into several sections. Label the sections as follows: Theory and Philosophy; Meditations and Practices; and Healing Techniques. Take notes

in them as you read this book. Use a separate section or notebook to record your experiences with the techniques, and a separate section for dreams and meditative insights that result from the exercises as they are performed.

2. Perform the simple purification practice at least once daily for five to ten minutes. Incorporate it into your daily spiritual practice.

3. Perform the purification practice and include a meditation on the nature of positive indifference and the benefits that it brings. Develop this quality within yourself through use of the following prayer: "I am in perfect harmony with all I experience today. Everything I experience is a message from the cosmos to me and is a teaching for my Illumination."

4. Perform the purification practice and include as your meditation on positive indifference a situation you have been in that upset you. Recreate it in your mind, changing only your emotional response to one of positive indifference. When you have gained experience with it, perform the meditation with an experience that made you feel good, but in a manner that was inflating to your ego.

5. Contact your local university or public library and see if they have *Encyclopedia of Religion*, *The Encyclopedia of Occultism and Parapsychology*, or the Brill *Dictionary of Gnosis and Western Esotericism*. If available, read the articles on alchemy, Kabbalah, Hermeticism, astrology, Rosicrucianism, the Hermetic Order of the Golden Dawn, theurgy, and Martinism.

Chapter 2

Kabbalistic Practice of Prayer, Meditation, and Ritual

Chapter Overview
- *Prayer, Meditation, and Ritual in Healing Practices*
- *Core Concepts in Western Esotericism*
- *The Lost Word and the Power of Creation*

In Kabbalah, there are three primary tools used to (1) experience heightened states of consciousness, (2) attune ourselves to the healing potential within and around us, and (3) create conditions in our life that are more productive and beneficial. These tools are prayer, meditation, and ritual. All esoteric systems use them to some degree, so it is important that each student take time to carefully utilize each of these tools in a balanced manner, thereby creating a sympathetic relationship between them for increased efficiency. The tendency to gravitate toward "what we like" or "what has meaning" for us is also the tendency to gravitate toward those things that reinforce our pathologies rather than bring them to the surface, address them, and integrate the raw material they represent. This is

"Whoever fixes a thing in his mind with complete firmness, that thing becomes for him the principle thing. Thus, when you pray and recite benedictions or wish to direct the prayer to something in a true manner, then imagine that you are light, and all about you is light from every direction, and every side. . . . And this illumination is inexhaustible and unending."

Sa'ar ha–Kawwanah,
attributed to Rabbi Azriel

particularly true when working as an individual without the guidance of more experienced associates or teachers.

A clear, simple, and regular practice can help us eliminate this problem and allow us to experience the emotional and physical health that we seek.

How to Use Prayer, Meditation, and Ritual in the Healing Practice

Prayer, meditation, and ritual are designed to reduce the friction in our daily, or objective, mind and allow it to merge first with our subjective or subconscious and, through it, realize the attunement it seeks.

> "The whole secret of prayer lies in this direction. Invoke often. Inflame thyself with prayer. It aims at moving the individual to ecstasy to transcend himself. In short, prayer consists of a complex of psychological and spiritual gestures . . . designed to enable us to recover our true identity, which is God."
>
> **Israel Regardie,**
> *The One Year Manual*

One of the cornerstones of Kabbalah, be it "kosher" or Hermetic, is that human beings can influence the hidden structure of the invisible worlds, the Godhead, and with proper intention and practice restore the harmony that is disrupted between the visible and invisible worlds—most importantly, between the physical world, human consciousness, and the mind of God.

A divine insight is possible, elevating each person who undertakes the work into ecstatic states, prophetic visions, and seemingly miraculous abilities to affect reality as it is understood. These energies can be brought down from the levels and worlds above the material, as well as directly from the source, or Nothingness, of the Ain Soph Aur. In Kabbalah, however, this is a fine line, as this connection to the Infinite is restored through prayer, meditation, and ritual, but more importantly through living a moral, upright, and righteous life. In short, traditional Kabbalah does not allow us to be unethical to our fellows while asking to be healed of our material, emotional, or physical ills. The basic commandments must be followed.

The function of meditation and prayer is identical—to attune the consciousness of the individual to the consciousness of God. In traditional esotericism, this process is refined and structured in such a way that the student may seek either a general oneness, often referred to as "cosmic consciousness" (Illumination), or attunement with a specific aspect, with nature, or with a nonhuman intelligence within the created universe—or even with another human being.

The subconscious aspect of our psyche is always in perfect attunement with the cosmos. Unfortunately for most people, they are only aware of this aspect of themselves under exceptional circumstances. As we will examine later, the Tree of Life, or all of creation, is focused in and through the subconscious mind. It is our daily objective mind that needs to be directed back toward Divinity, or, in Kabbalah, the Limitless Light.

The subconscious part of our being is concerned with the autonomic functions of the body as well as habituation of the mind in terms of thoughts, feelings, and images. The subconscious acts as the collection point of our every emotion and all of the images, ideas, and physical actions we ever experience. It has no reasoning capability but is synthetic, cyclic, and reactive in its application and unlimited in its power. The subconscious is the key to all magic and the gateway to initiation beyond material life. It is also, based on how we use it, the gatekeeper of heaven or hell.

We say "back toward Divinity" because our central sense of Self, which feels itself to be the center of the universe, is in reality completely absorbed for the majority of people in the daily concerns of incarnation—the world around them. They have no real experience of the inner world or of the subtle forces at work in this one.

Only in times of rest and sleep, or even chemical influence and illness, does the central sense of Self for the majority of people get a hint of something "other" than the hard world of material life.

When this happens, we can either continue this experience in the realm of "other" or run toward material consciousness for a temporary respite from the inner realities that await us.

The significance of this is that while human consciousness exists independent of external realities, it is yet projected into the material domain to gain experience of friction and duality. This is not its normal, or even sole, realm of realization. This situation creates a crisis for many people. They can hide from the spiritual realities by focusing only on material realities, or they can run from physical life and enter the denser spiritual realms through artificial means, stress-induced psychotic episodes, or even sleep brought on by depression. And yet in many ways, material life, for a weak and fledgling conscious being, is safe, stable, and easy to work with and identify with. It appears that to fully enter into either world and be victorious requires strength, commitment, and one-pointed focus.

Distinctions

Prayer is a kind of dialogue between the inner and outer parts of self, or a "word bridge" that unites these seemingly separated parts of our awareness. In fact, it is false even to speak of "parts of our awareness" as if we are fractured or broken beings. In truth, we become aware of whatever we focus our mind on. By focusing our mind on psychic or spiritual matters, we simply become more aware of them.

Meditation is focusing the mind or consciousness on a single idea. This is usually composed of an image, symbol, or word. From this focusing of the mind, a sense of unity develops between the various aspects of consciousness as they are brought to bear on a single point.

Meditations consist of two kinds: static and dynamic. *Static* is focusing on a single idea; *dynamic* is allowing that idea to unfold, or assisting it through multiple serial symbols. In Kabbalah, dynamic meditation is often called Pathworking.

There is no "repair" or actual "uniting." These words reflect the limits of conventional vocabulary to reflect the experiences that esotericism offers. Closer to the truth is the Eastern idea of "cleaning" or "uncovering." That is, we remove the obstacles—be they emotional or intellectual—that prevent us from experiencing the inner life. It is no different than moving a chair that blocks a door so that we may go through. Nothing miraculous happens, but it feels that way as we enter into the new room and see all it has to offer or meet whomever is inside.

By strengthening our mental muscles of concentration and visualization, we are able to "move" the obstacles—fleeting thoughts, random emotions, indecisiveness, and so on—that prevent us from experiencing the inner life. When this is accomplished, a greater harmony is developed between our interior and exterior experiences, our aspirations and our actual results.

Prayer is slightly different from meditation, yet it seeks to achieve the same goal. While centuries of esoteric and mainstream religious practices have demonstrated what constitutes the effectiveness of prayer, science has established repeatedly that prayer is effective in promoting the healing of animals and humans, and even in the growth of plants.

1. Verbal prayer is more effective than praying mentally; that is why it is suggested that all sacred chants, sounds, divine names, or words of power be intoned whenever possible. In the purification practice previously given, the difference between an internal and silent confession versus a clearly spoken one will be immediately noticed.

2. Stretching out the hands in blessing over the person, place, or thing being prayed for increases the effectiveness of the prayer. Through physical acts and gestures, be they simple or part of more complex rituals, we unite our inner intention with our outer expression, thereby giving it life.

3. Visualization of the existence of the thing or state while praying aids in the effectiveness of prayer. Clearly knowing what we are seeking to achieve or experience makes it all that much easier to do and brings integration and harmony to our life. Here the fruits of meditation previously discussed can be transferred to the prayer process. This visualization can be either literal or symbolic.

Symbols

William Butler Yeats, in his essay *Magic*, published in 1901, stated that he believed the following points were the foundation of all magical practices from the earliest of antiquity:

1. "That the borders of the mind are ever shifting, and that many minds can flow into one another, as it were, and create or reveal a single mind, a single energy."

2. "That the borders of our memories are ever shifting, and that our memories are part of one great memory, the memory of Nature herself."

3. "That this great mind and great memory can be evoked by symbols."[1]

---

1 Quoted in: R. A. Gilbert, *The Golden Dawn Scrapbook* (York Beach, ME: Weiser, 1997), 176.

Symbols are the "language of the soul," referred to in alchemy as the "language of the birds." Birds such as the dove, the hawk, the ibis, and the mysterious benu bird are found in Jewish and Egyptian symbolism as representations of immortal consciousness. It is also well known to students of esotericism that King Solomon is revered by Jews and Arabs alike as being a great magician for his knowing the "language of the birds." This is a poetic way of saying that Solomon understood the language of the soul, the inner voice of intuition.

Symbols reflect the geographic and historical experience of the people and traditions using them. That is why it can be confusing and counterproductive to mix symbols from different systems in an attempt to create a single, all-encompassing multicultural method. Each system is complete within itself. Pick one and become familiar with it before adding to or deleting from it. To do otherwise is to be a dilettante at best and, at worst, to send confusing messages to the subconscious (the source of psychic power) and guarantee frustration and failure.

Symbols too often rely on anthropomorphic images, which creates a problem when encountering the forces they represent. The human tendency to take symbols literally, especially when they are in human form, created the injunctions against idols found in both Judaism and Islam. This forced the adherents of these faiths to think and reason more abstractly and less concretely than many neighboring cults, which allowed symbols to be used to represent abstract forces, intelligences, and consciousness, such as the *sigillia* of Agrippa, Paracelsus, and their contemporaries. These linear figures are used to act as "seals" in the mind and aura of the operator, and they are often used in the creation of talismans. They have a powerful effect when impressed upon the psychic body or aura of a recipient, bringing to action a host of related energies.

Types of Rituals

In traditional settings, Kabbalah would be understood in the context of Jewish religious celebrations, and by Christian Kabbalists, primarily in relation to the Catholic Mass and related holiday services. For Hermeticists, social structure required attendance at public religious services, as well as a public declaration of faith. As such, Hermeticists would interpret Kabbalah in light of common religious worship as well as Hermetic philosophy and related occult practices. Modern Kabbalah is primarily Hermetic and interprets the tradition in accordance with occult rituals and practices.

From an esoteric perspective, the function of ritual is to assist the mind by creating a symbolic context of several layers, often involving physical representations of those symbols, to enhance the engagement of the physical senses, which aids in altering consciousness. All rituals fall into one of two types: (1) to increase the available energy in order to raise consciousness to the point of absorption in a preselected idea (invocation), and (2) to increase the available energy in order to create a context for bringing an idea into psychic or even material manifestation (evocation).

This process of invocation and evocation are used in four specific ways:

1. **Initiation Rituals**—These are designed to induce specific states of awareness.
2. **Consecrations**—Talismans, ritual tools, Eucharistic.
3. **Evocations**—Visible manifestation of an invisible intelligence or force.
4. **Healings**—This includes the physical body as well as the subconscious, the removal of an obstacle or block in the psyche, and even the extremely rare instance of exterior invasion of the psyche of an individual by outside forces in the form of an exorcism.

Attunement to an energy, idea, planet, sphere, or ritual celebration such as a Mass could be considered a ritual in itself; however, this is also a prerequisite for any ritual to be successful.

All rituals, like a fine piece of music or work of literature, have at least three parts: an opening, a middle part or reason for the ritual, and a closing.

The middle section of a ritual can be as simple or complex as desired. For healing work and general spiritual practices, it is desirable to keep the middle simple and to the point.

Opening—Preparation of the mind, clearing of obstacles to the work.

Middle—Intention, purpose of the ritual.

Closing—Completion of the work, causeway to normal consciousness.

The Eucharistic elements of a ritual, such as the charging of water or food, are similar to the consecration of a talisman or ritual object, with the exception that the Eucharist is consumed during the ritual and is not stored for later use. While the phrase "consecration of a talisman" may be unfamiliar to some, it can simply be seen as similar to charging a crystal or gemstone for healing purposes, only in a more formal and ritualistic setting.

Rituals may also feature vitalizing and charging of psychic centers, with the Middle Pillar Exercise being the principal method in modern Western magical schools. However, the Middle Pillar has technical limits as far as most schools have taught it. Information in *Kabbalah for Health & Wellness* addresses these limits, making the Middle Pillar Exercise more effective, particularly for healing work.

A ritual can also be seen as a kind of repetitive action that allows the practitioner to free the focus from conscious thought and enter into an altered state. This kind of ritual is usually not ceremonial in nature, with candles, invocations, and so on, as these require a great deal of attention on what is being done. Rather, they are more akin to a well-practiced form of self-hypnosis in which rhythmic motions, tapping, chanting, or counting are used. Through the influence of suggestion, words, gestures, environment, and even thought (telepathy), individuals can be directed into subtle and profound states of receptivity for healing work. These kinds of practices are the foundation of the shamanic journey and form a common foundation across cultures and settings. Shamanism as the predecessor of traditional practices such as Kabbalah, alchemy, and astrology is too often ignored. This failure to integrate practical, simple techniques into modern Hermetic practice is a tragic failure to meet the needs of the average seeker. This book seeks to rectify this weakness and demonstrate that there are very real forms of practice that are identical to early shamanic practices and are also useful to the modern student. The most common form of Hermetic or Kabbalistic "shamanism" can be found in the central European and German practices of "brauche," or "pow-wow," as it is called in the United States. Pow-wow is deeply rooted in Renaissance and pre-Renaissance magical practices and focuses mainly on healing humans and animals and protection of property, crops, and personal life and limb.

Pow-wow is still practiced today in parts of German-American communities rooted in traditional religious and agricultural practices. These include the Amish, Mennonites, and even Lutherans and Dunkards who are near the edge of those areas geographically.

It has been stated that the three principal methods used in traditional Western esotericism are:

1. Pronunciation of divine names.

2. Identification with deific, or divine, forms.

3. Invocation and banishing of forces.

To these it might be added:

4. Continuous identification with a chosen divine form as a form of perpetual prayer.

5. Perceiving the physical world as an expression of the spiritual and, as such, a habitat of the gods.

It is important to create a condition within oneself that allows for the fullness of life to be experienced and to flow. Simply going through the motions of a ritual will make it a habit, but not a very effective one. To be effective, ritual must be an action that allows us to contact the emotional energy behind the symbols being used and to transfer this energy to the unconscious for manifestation in the material world and for opening gateways to higher consciousness:

> Ritual, with its symbolic enactment of the cosmic drama, can go a long way but cannot go the whole way. It can provide dietary supplement that will enable the undernourished to keep alive, but it will not give the bounding energy of real health. As a means to an end the symbolic ritual is admirable; as an end in itself it is a compromise and makeshift; better than nothing but not the genuine article. It cannot, moreover, be worked satisfactorily by those who themselves are obliged to rely on substitutes for life in its fullness. Those who possess fullness of life can mediate to others by means of ritual; but if they themselves suffer from restriction or inhibition of life force, they can no more mediate the cosmic life to those for whose benefit they work a ritual than a starving mother can feed her baby.[2]

---

2 Dion Fortune and Gareth Knight, *The Circuit of Force* (Loughbrough, UK: Thoth Publications, 1998).

Some summary points to remember:

- All rituals act as a container or filter for the energies of the subconscious.
- Rituals have the subconscious as their primary field of activity, helping to bring things into consciousness or into material manifestation.
- Rituals act as a medium or gateway and become unnecessary once their goal is achieved.
- Rituals do not act directly on either the spiritual or physical aspects, but rather are creations of the mind to direct, channel, control, and express in a specific manner the energies of the unconscious.

The Power of Positive Thinking

Positive thinking is the most important tool Kabbalists, Hermeticists, or alchemists must have if any of their activities are to turn their studies from intellectual abstractions into working interior experiences. If you generate confidence, goodwill, compassion, generosity, and assuredness of success prior to all activities, be they mundane or esoteric (for there is no real difference at some point), then the desired goals of peace, well-being, prosperity, and, above all, Illumination will be yours.

It would be wrong to dismiss rituals, prayers, talismans, and similar props as simply confidence-building devices. While for the beginner they certainly fulfill that need, to the advanced practitioner, even the adept, they are external expressions of an inner state—visible tools for an invisible force, wielded together through the skillful application of consciousness.

While it can be argued that such tools are not necessary for the successful undertaking of the work, such a statement is based more in theory than in practice. It is not essential to have a hammer or saw to build a house, but certainly such tools make it more beautiful, as well as easier and more enjoyable to build than without tools. The same is true with our "inner constructions" as well.

The Power of the Word

Because a positive attitude is critical to the effective work of occult operations, it is imperative that we only speak in positive terms when dealing with life issues—and even more so when we write about them—as in doing so we invoke the power of "the Word," or the primordial creative power within us. This "Word," or *Verbum* in Latin, is the fundamental means of creation written about in the first verse of the first chapter of the Gospel of John, "In principio erat Verbum" (In the beginning was the Word), and in the fourteenth verse, "Et Verbum caro factum est" (And the Word was made flesh).

Once creation took on motion and became form, this original sound or Word was lost. That is, it went from being a purely spiritual expression of creative power to becoming a material manifestation. Once form was made, the energy the Word contained was locked into a specific expression and was said to have become lost in the silence and stillness of matter. Retrieving this original power to create from pure energy in the world of matter and to release the energy in matter back to the world of form is called "the Search for the Lost Word" in some schools and "the Great Work" in others.

However, the power of the Word is not completely lost. Each person contains the power of creation within and uses it constantly. Either it is used consciously, deliberately, and with skill, or it is used unconsciously, haphazardly, and improperly. The principal means of expressing this power, of setting in motion vast and powerful forces in our psyche, is speech. Speech affects our own psyche, stimulating our unconscious to action, fulfilling our stated words as well as those around us, adding their psychic power and influence to our life. Negative speech must be rooted out, for by rooting it out we are closer to rooting out our negative emotions. By eliminating our negative emotions, we give room and

"Much is achieved by our mind through faith, which is a firm belief, a fixed intention, and a complete absorption of the operator or recipient, and it assists in every matter and lends strength to every deed we wish to do; so that what may be called an image is formed inside us of the power to be assimilated and of the thing to be performed in us or by us. Therefore in every work and application we must employ a strong desire, must stretch our imagination, and must have the most sanguine hope and the firmest faith, for this contributes very much to success. . . .

Thus in order to perform magic, firm faith and unbounded confidence are required; there must not be the slightest doubt of success or the least thought of failure. For just as, even on those occasions when the wrong procedure is used, a firm and unshakable faith can do wonders."

Cornelius Agrippa,
Three Books of Occult Philosophy,
Chapter LXVI

expression to our positive life-affirming power. This is why engaging in regular purification practices is critically important, particularly prior to formal meditation or ritual sessions. Through these practices and control over our speech, we can begin to continuously generate positive and constructive energy.

From our controlled speech we also begin to work backward toward controlling our thoughts and our physical actions, so that they reinforce our desired inner state.

The same is true when assisting others who are ill. By understanding patients' speech, we understand their psychology or dominant view as well as their illness as an expression of that view. This also gives us the keys to assist them in understanding and correcting both their inner and outer disharmony.

Technique—A Basic Technique for Prayer

Explanation—Prayer should be simple and direct and should use only as much structure as is needed to commune with our Inner Self.

Type of Practice—This practice can be done in conjunction with any meditation, ritual, or healing practice you may undertake. It is a core practice.

Preparation—Sit comfortably with your back straight, your feet flat on the floor, the palms of your hands flat on your thighs and close to your hips (to take stress off your shoulders and elbows), and your chin slightly tucked. Breathe deeply several times, hold your breath for as long as is comfortable, exhale slowly, and hold your breath out for as long as is comfortable. Feel yourself relax mentally, emotionally, and physically as you do this. Imagine that you are made of light and that your body is empty except for radiant light. Perform the purification practice given in chapter 1.

Method—Proceed as follows:

1. After you have completed the purification practice, allow yourself and any sense of self to dissolve into the light that surrounds you.

2. Dwell in this light; rest in it.

3. When you feel ready, begin your prayer, or your dialogue with God. Sense that a divine energy or presence is all around you and that it is hearing what you are saying.

4. Begin with an expression of heartfelt gratitude and confession of your errors, actual or perceived, and forgiveness for those who have wronged you or whom you perceive as having wronged you. This is important. Without first simply being aware of the preciousness of your very existence, as well as an admission of error, desire to correct it, and forgiveness for others, there is no way that you can approach God in sincerity and truth. Then, if you have something particular for which you are looking for advice, assistance, or direct action, be specific and, if possible, visualize the desired outcome. Be clear and to the point; otherwise, you may get the result you are after, but you will be unaware of it because of your fuzzy attitude.

5. Finally, ask for guidance and assistance at every moment of every day, and ask that you may be a fitting coworker in the divine plan, human evolution, the Illumination of others, or however you want to phrase it. When this is complete, rest in the light. Simple breathing can assist this process a great deal.

Incorporation into Daily Life—Prayer is the easiest and most direct method for spiritual development and communion with the cosmos. It knows no limits in its application and can be undertaken anywhere at any time without inconvenience or need for extensive privacy.

Technique—A Basic Technique for Meditation

Explanation—Meditation is simple and easy when properly understood. The following method is the basis for all the techniques in this book and will allow the average person to quickly and easily experience deep states of relaxation and concentration with little or no effort.

Type of Practice—Core practice.

Preparation—Prepare yourself as in the previous two exercises. Perform the purification practice.

Method—Proceed as follows:

1. Breathe slowly and deeply through your nose.

2. Imagine your diaphragm, feet, and body as a sponge soaking up the energy.

3. Focus only on your breath. Give a 60/40 split on your concentration: about 60 percent on the breathing and 40 percent on the image, symbol, and so on. This may shift, and that is OK.

4. When done, stand up, stretch, and clap your hands loudly once, stamp your left foot, or ring a small bell or gong to focus your attention in the material world.

Incorporation into Daily Practice—This can be done daily, even for as few as three to five minutes.

At this point, it is easy to tie these three techniques together into a seamless daily practice: (1) purification practice, (2) period of prayer, and (3) meditating on a specific topic or simply resting in the light induced by the initial period of prayer through breathing.

A Basic Ritual for Daily Use: Attuning to the Tradition

Every spiritual tradition has its form of what Buddhism calls "taking refuge." In taking refuge, practicing Buddhists state that until they achieve enlightenment, they draw their strength, support, and teachings from their *guru* (teacher), the *dharma* (teachings), and the *sanga* (community).

Christians find salvation in Christ, which is commonly done through the aid of a priest or clergy person who gives teachings on the faith, as well as in the collective "Body of Christ," which is the sum of the invisible church, the corporate church, and the body of believers with whom one participates in the sacraments.

Judaism has the rabbi (teacher), who studies the Torah (teachings) and dispenses and encourages study of the teachings, and the congregation of participants in the synagogue, who as Jews are part of the "chosen people" of God.

Freemasonry has the Master of the Lodge, the Book of the Sacred Law, and the Lodge membership, referred to as "the Household of the faithful."

Alchemy has the master or adept, the secret teachings (oral, written, and symbolic), and the initiatic line of which each alchemist is a member.

Occult and mystical lodges have their variations on the theme, but in the end, it all comes down to identifying with fellow practitioners, the teachings, and the living expression of those teachings in the form of the teacher.

Even if seekers do not have a teacher from whom they are learning, they can still identify with the living traditions of alchemy, Hermeticism, and Kabbalah. This kind of practice is a deep-seated expression of gratitude and recognition of the historical link of events that had brought each of us to the Path. Without this kind of reflection and without appreciation for those who have assisted us, even if imperfectly, we are incapable of further progress. More will be said on this in chapter 7 in the exercise for awakening the Inner Master; until then, it is sufficient for each of us to meditate on these ideas and to perform the following simple ritual for daily attunement to the Hermetic tradition.

Prayer, meditation, and ritual work together in spiritual practices, as prayer establishes the purpose or intent of the activity, ritual establishes the context of the activity, and meditation establishes the content, or the inner work that anchors tangibly to intangible ideas and energies.

Practice—Ritual of Attunement to the Tradition

Explanation—The following ritual is designed so that anyone can perform it and derive a deeper connection to the various traditions of Western esotericism. Have available an image or picture of Thoth-Tahuti, the Egyptian god and traditional guardian of Western esotericism. An image of the Tree of Life or the Philosopher's Stone will also do.

Type of Practice—This is a preliminary practice that can be done after any sacred space has been created and prior to any general meditations or healing work, so that we may draw upon the collective energy, wisdom, and presence of the tradition to assist us in our work.

Preparation—Sit comfortably with your back straight, your feet flat on the floor, the palms of your hands flat on your thighs and close to your hips (to take stress off your shoulders and elbows), and your chin slightly tucked. Breathe deeply several times, hold your breath for as long as is comfortable, exhale slowly, and hold your breath out for as long as is comfortable. Feel yourself relax mentally, emotionally, and physically as you do this. Taking our hint from Rabbi Azriel in the quote at the beginning of this chapter, let's each prepare ourselves for prayer by creating a proper mental and emotional state. Visualization helps us do this and is an important tool in esoteric practices regardless of their nature. For our purposes, we will use the purification practice given in chapter 1.

Method—Proceed as follows:

1. Imagine before you in space the figure of Thoth-Tahuti. If you are a Christian Hermeticist, Jesus Christ can be used. If you are Jewish and want a more kosher approach, use a sphere or brilliant point of light.

2. Surrounding the image are six spheres of light, and a white brilliance emanates from the central figure. You can imagine these spheres of light as the seven archangels if you like, or as the various figures of Hermetic tradition—Roger Bacon, Nicholas and Perenelle Flamel, Mistress Maria, Cagliostro and his wife, St. Germain—or even modern proponents, such as those of the Golden Dawn, Martinism, Rosicrucianism, and so on. The spheres receive their energy from the central sphere or figure and radiate energy back toward it. After a minute or two, they collapse into the central figure, and it grows brighter. Imagine it reducing in size, retaining its brilliance, and entering into the top of your head and resting in your heart. Feel its energies spread throughout your entire being.

3. As you grow comfortable with this exercise, you can imagine the spheres as brilliant colored light and as located in the directions below. You can add their complementary colors as a highlight, or use the complementary colors to form the planetary symbol (or Hebrew letter) associated with the corresponding sphere. The following information is taken from the *Sepher Yetzirah*: front—east, Venus, green; behind—west, Jupiter, blue; right—south, Sun, golden; left—north, Mars, red; above—

Mercury, orange; below—Moon, violet; center—Saturn, black. Have the outer spheres line up to form an axis through your heart.

4. Rest in this feeling of connection to the great traditions, and know that you can call upon these teachers, guides, and invisible powers to assist you when you need to. You also must be willing to assist them and work for the Illumination of others as well as yourself. In this, you become one of the links in the great invisible chain of "the tradition."

Incorporation into Daily Practice—The structure and purpose of this simple ritual is clear: it can easily be modified to meet the needs of a specific school or practice (such as fitting exclusively alchemy or being more kosher). Regardless of structure, the most important thing is that we identify with those who have come before us on the Path and recognize our relationship and our debt to them, as well as be willing to carry the tradition forward in service to others. Without this commitment, the tradition would simply die with us, and the efforts of our ancestors would be wasted on our selfishness.

Practice—The Six Directions

Explanation—This practice is more general than the previous one and is designed for general use. It is short and simple and can even be done as a preliminary to the Ritual of Attunement to the Tradition. Before we can enter into various altered states or dimensions, we need to establish where we are in time and space as well as our relationship to them. The following practice is ideal as a preparatory practice for additional meditations or as a stand-alone practice. It is easier and simpler than the pentagram rituals that are often used, fulfills the same function, and in some ways is more potent in its anchoring the energies involved into the psychic and physical bodies of the operator.

Type of Practice—Preliminary practice to establish a sacred space for meditation, prayer, or healing work or to attune with the elements and balance them within oneself.

Preparation—Two to three minutes of relaxation as previously described.

Method—Once preparations are completed, proceed as follows:

1. Prepare yourself by sitting straight in a chair, shoulders relaxed, chin tucked, and palms resting on your thighs. Breathing is slow, deep, and relaxed.

2. Visualize a sphere of brilliant light about a foot above your head. This is the primordial ground of Being, the first impulse of manifestation from the unmanifest realms of the Nothingness. Imagine a line comes down from it, through you, and into the earth beneath you, forming there a brilliant obsidian-black sphere. This new sphere is a foundational essence of material creation. It is physical life as we know it.

3. Imagine a sharp, brilliant yellow sphere with violet highlights about three feet in front of you. Place the symbol of elemental air in it (if you do not know this symbol, see the chart on page 48). This sphere is air, or the gaseous nature of creation. It is the source of consciousness and life as we know it. It binds all of creation together.

4. Imagine a line of light moving from the sphere through you to form a brilliant and sharp blue sphere with orange highlights about three feet behind you. Place the symbol for elemental water in this sphere (this symbol appears in the chart on page 48). This is primordial water, the source of all psychic and emotional expression. It is also the womb of all material creation.

5. Imagine a brilliant red sphere with emerald green highlights about three feet to your right. Place the symbol for elemental fire in this sphere (this symbol appears in the chart on page 48). This is primordial fire, the source of energy and individuality in creation. Fire allows us to become more self-aware, as well as to move, change, create, and transmute situations, qualities, and energies within and outside of ourselves.

6. Imagine a line of light moving from the red sphere through you (forming a cross at or about the level of your heart, where the previous line went) to about three feet to your left, forming there a brilliant emerald green sphere with red highlights. Place the symbol for elemental earth in this sphere (this symbol appears in the chart on page 48). This is primordial earth, or solidity. It is the basis of consciousness, in that

without solidity, consciousness would not have anything to express itself through.

7. Starting with air in front of you, link all of the spheres with a circle, moving first to fire on your right, then water behind you, then to earth on your left, and finishing back at air.

8. As you progress, this line need not be entirely distinct, but should form more or less a sphere around you. The feeling of being enclosed in a distinct space with these six energetic points is what is being developed, rather than a specific visualization of traditional ritual circles.

9. Now, locate the point at or near your heart where the lines intersect. Concentrate on this point. Feel it radiate as a brilliant point of consciousness, of light, reaching out and connecting with the six spheres you just created and placed in the six directions. Rest in this central point of stability for a minute or so, and then begin your daily meditation or prayer session.

You may want to do a small invocation of each of the directions as you visualize them. The following is based on traditional prayers of the same sort that are common in Kabbalah, as well as across many folk systems of magic. Some of you will notice its distinct similarity to the famous "St. Patrick's Breastplate."

"Primordial Light Above Me!
Ground of my Being Beneath Me!
Air of Wisdom Before Me!
Water of Life Behind Me!
Fire of Self at My Right Hand!
Earth of Nature at My Left Hand!
Self of Self in the Center, Uniting the Whole!"

Of course, you are free to create your own prayer insofar as it addresses the essential qualities and elements presented. Once you get familiar with the process, you may want to add additional qualities to the visualization to deepen your understanding of this simple ritual as well as to strengthen your results from it. Hebrew divine names of God are associated with each of the directions as well and may be incorporated as you progress. It is best to "make haste slowly" and layer new material onto well-integrated experiences.

Incorporation into Daily Practice—This practice should be done at least once a week, or you may use a suitable substitute, such as the well-known pentagram rituals.

Direction	Color	Element	Divine Name	Quality	Symbol	Letter
Above	Brilliant white	Void/Spirit +	Ehieh	Active Spirit	•	Ayin
Below	Black	Void/Spirit −	Agla	Passive Spirit	•	Tau
Before	Yellow/Violet	Air/Ruach	YHVH	Ideas/Framework	△	Vau
Behind	Blue/Orange	Water/Maim	El	Emotions/Psychic	▽	Heh
Right	Red/Green	Fire/Aesh	Elohim	Energy/Action	△	Yod
Left	Green/Red	Earth/Aretz	Adoni	Form/Expression	▽	Heh
Center	Clear/Diamond	Spirit	YHShVH/IAO	Balance/Potential	⊛	Shin
Sphere	Bluish white	Spirit	None	Unites all parts	None	None

Key Points

- Prayer, meditation, and ritual are the three main tools for spiritual attunement.

- Prayer, often misunderstood in contemporary esoteric circles, is the fastest, easiest, and most direct method.

- Meditation allows us to open to the inner voice of our intuition and Inner Master.

- Ritual creates a powerful emotionally and symbolically rich environment for awakening to take place in.

- Symbols and ideas are rooted in traditions and history. To attempt to remove them from their context and use them in a culturally free environment is to do violence to both the system and culture.

- Systems are attuned to, and relationships are developed, over time. They are not vehicles that one simply gets into, drives for a while, and then trades in.

- Skill, success, understanding, and Illumination are the result of consistent, dedicated, and focused work, both in material and in spiritual matters.

Assignments for Chapter 2

1. Perform the Ritual of Attunement to the Tradition daily for at least two weeks. Using the Internet and other research tools, find images, photographs, or paintings of the following historical and mythological figures for inclusion: Hermes, Thoth, St. Germain (see the works of Manly P. Hall for an accurate depiction), Cagliostro and his wife, Nicholas and Perenelle Flamel, Roger Bacon, Michael Maier, Paracelsus, Abulafia, King Solomon, Reuchlin, Marsillio Ficino, Israel Regardie, Frater Albertus, MacGregor Mathers, and other modern and contemporary authorities who have made the Hermetic tradition or one or more of its subtopics the major area of their life's work.

2. Spend several weeks developing this image of the tradition, its masters, and your relationship to it.

3. Incorporate the Ritual of Attunement to the Tradition with the Six Directions into your daily practice.

4. Spend time meditating on each of the ideas and energies presented by the individual components of the Six Directions: active Spirit (consciousness), passive Spirit (universal presence), air (intelligence/organization), fire (energy), water (emotions, psychic energy), earth (solidity, structure, matter), and center (harmonization of all the elements within oneself).

Chapter 3

The Sepher Yetzirah *and the Tree of Life*

Chapter Overview
- *The Book of Formation*
- *The Tree of Life and Ten Levels of Creation*
- *The Power of Hebrew Letters and Their Use in Healing*

The *Sepher Yetzirah* (Book of Formation) is one of the most enigmatic and yet useful books in Kabbalistic literature. Enigmatic in that while several versions exist,[1] it is essentially a small book, describing creation and the relationship between the Hebrew letters and a host of correspondences. It is these correspondences that set the *Sepher Yetzirah* as the major linchpin in synthesizing an array of Kabbalistic doctrines, theories, and practices, making it the most widely circulated and utilized meditation manual in Kabbalistic literature.

Regardless of geography, the ancients interpreted invisible phenomena into the visible world through a series of complex relationships called correspondences. This idea of correspondences is key to all forms of ancient and Renaissance sympathetic magic as well as modern New Age energetic healing modalities. It states that from the most subtle realm of Nothingness (Ain Soph Aur) to the greatest material density (Malkuth),

1 Aryeh Kaplan's *Sefer Yetzirah: The Book of Creation* gives several versions of the text, providing extensive commentary on the meditative process as well as the translation. Charts for comparison of similarities and differences make Kaplan's book invaluable.

there is a continuous stream of ideas, energy, colors, shapes, sounds, and symbols that are interacting with each other, and by knowing what they are and how they relate, we can affect the flow of energy.[2] The *Sepher Yetzirah* supplies Kabbalists with a set of correspondences that form the basis for their work in spiritual and physical healing.

The Book of Formation

The *Sepher Yetzirah* (Book of Formation) describes three things of interest to practical Kabbalah:

- The Cube of Space
- The Tree of Life
- The correspondences between the Hebrew alphabet and creation

In addition, it contains several meditative exercises with no clearly defined function but which, through their abstract design, improve concentration, visualization, and receptivity to subtle influences and insights.

The *Cube of Space* is a three-dimensional model of the formation of "space," or the initial creative matrix, out of a one- and two-dimensional reality. This "cube" is created as specific sounds are formed, thereby moving energy into specific patterns and creating what we know as space. The Hebrew alphabet is used to represent these primordial sounds, and in fact, it is given the designation as being the "language of the angels" as a result. According to Kabbalistic theory, through the proper pronunciation of these sounds, a person can effect creation. Each letter is located on the Cube either on one of the six faces, in the center, or at the angles. (The keys to the six faces on the opposite page are labeled as if from inside the Cube; the letter Tau is in the center.) Modern Hermetic schools have also given an association of the tarot cards to the Cube through their letter correspondences.

---

2 Experiments have been made in physics in which the attitude, or even presence, of the scientists performing the experiments have affected the outcome. There is compelling evidence that electrons and other subatomic particles or "quanta" behave as particles *only when we are observing them*; otherwise, they behave as a wave. This means that the building blocks of the universe only coagulate when being observed, and afterward they return to the energy-matter soup behind everything we experience: in short, consciousness affects matter.

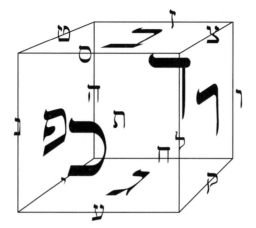

Kabbalistic Cube of Space

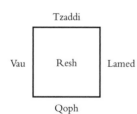

	Zayin	
Heh	Daleth	Vau
	Cheth	

East Face

	Teth	
Nun	Peh	Heh
	Yod	

North Face

	Tzaddi	
Vau	Resh	Lamed
	Qoph	

South Face

	Samekh	
Lamed	Kaph	Nun
	Ayin	

West Face

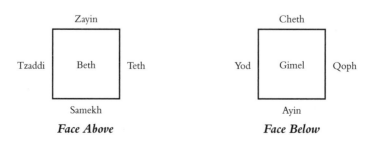

	Zayin	
Tzaddi	Beth	Teth
	Samekh	

Face Above

	Cheth	
Yod	Gimel	Qoph
	Ayin	

Face Below

The Tree of Life

Creation is seen to have taken place, in Kabbalistic (and Hermetic-alchemical) terms, in the following process:

The divine mind of God, the Absolute Nothingness (also known as the Limitless Light), through a series of expansions and contractions, establishes the boundaries of creation. The first world is the most subtle and is closest to the original state of nonexistence, and it is *Atziluth*. This is called the World of Fire, because of the lively, undefined, and almost uncontrollable nature of fire. Next is *Briah*, or the World of Archetypes and forms as our human mind grasps them. It is symbolized as the World of Air, and as a result it is a barrier world that is formed by the creation of the next world, *Yetzirah*, or the World of Water. This is the highly psychic and emotionally charged world immediately behind the veil of material existence, or *Assiah* (action). Assiah is also known as the World of Earth, because of the solid, concrete nature of material life.[3]

One Tree, Four Worlds

The doctrine of involution and evolution is important to Hermetic thought, but we will skip a detailed explanation, as it is not essential to energetic healing practices. In summary, it states that the energy-matter-consciousness nucleus grows denser and less powerful as it moves from unity (Kether) to materialization (Malkuth), and that the various stages involved create the intermediary spheres of the Tree of Life. It is the purpose of each being (Adam) to go from "blissful ignorance" (Paradise) into ignorance (the Fall) and, in the experiences found in material existence, return to their primordial state (New Jerusalem) but with total knowledge, wisdom, and power. It is the story of the Prodigal Son as told in the New Testament.

As unity emanates and creates the various levels of energy-matter-consciousness we call the Tree of Life, it also creates several reflections of it, each with its own unique expression of those energies. The first Tree, if we could call it that, is mostly energy, little mind, virtually no form, and

---

3 Some schools will place the order as fire, water, air, and earth. Hermetic and alchemical schools utilize the order given in this chapter. The *Sepher Yetzirah* is clear in the order of generation—fire, water, air—but it also states that air comes between fire and water. Both models work. Remember, "The map is not the territory."

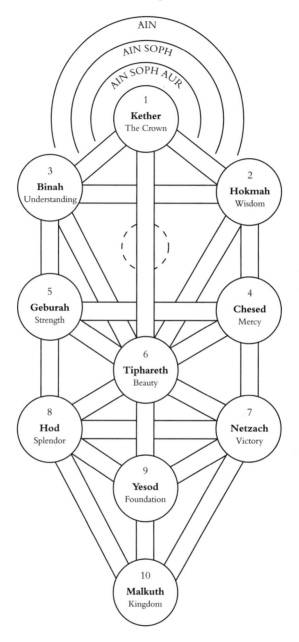

The Tree of Life

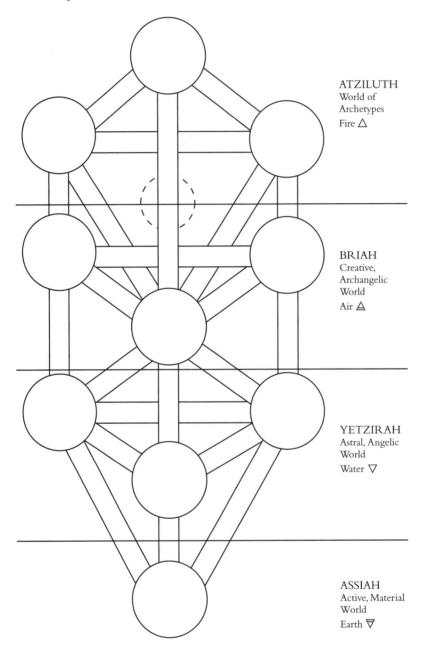

ATZILUTH
World of
Archetypes
Fire △

BRIAH
Creative,
Archangelic
World
Air △

YETZIRAH
Astral, Angelic
World
Water ▽

ASSIAH
Active, Material
World
Earth ▽

The Four Kabbalistic Worlds

no matter (at least as we would understand it). This is the Tree of Atziluth, of the Spiritual World, and because of its energetic nature it is often associated with fire, or Yod in the Tetragrammaton—the sacred and mysterious divine name of God in Hebrew.

The second reflection, emanating from the completion of the first, imitates this process and creates another Tree. This second Tree takes the minute and highly discrete and distinct energy pulses that create the seed Sephiroth in the first Tree and turns them into discrete and distinct ideas. These ideas are still broad and encompass many subsets, and they are abstract in that they are more archetypes than "facts." Platonic solids and geometric forms are a perfect expression of the spheres as they relate to this Tree. This Tree is process-oriented in nature, and it is often associated with air and the first Heh in the Tetragrammaton.

A third Tree is created in the same fashion as the second, and it takes the abstract ideas of shape and thought and turns them into powerful emotions, feelings, instincts, and concrete images. This Tree is associated with the domain of water, for water is what gives life and physical form to creation, and with the letter Vau of the Tetragrammaton.

The fourth and final Tree is created in identical fashion to the previous ones, only it is dense, hard, material, and concrete. It gives rise to, and is tangible to, the physical senses. This world moves from its own point of near-nonexistence, the First Swirlings, to the universe as we know it. This physical universe is the World of Assiah, action, and is associated with the final Heh of the Tetragrammaton. It is here, in the material world, that the abstract ideas and ideals of consciousness are worked out and made manifest.

Each human being has his or her own Tree within the aura. This Tree connects us to the larger Tree, or Trees, and holds the seed energies of our evolution. The awakening, directing, and expression of these seed energies, in harmony with their spiritual source, is the work of each Kabbalist.

These energies also express themselves in a unique fashion, in that as our physical body (Guph) connects us to the physical earth (Malkuth), it is Malkuth that connects us to the broader physical universe (Assiah).

The etheric energies that make up the physical body are also shared by our nervous system, our instinctual need to create (libido), and our subconscious mind. Just as our nervous system connects our consciousness to the material world and our libido connects us to another human being (to continue the species), our subconscious connects us to the emotions, instincts, and thoughts in our immediate environment and, if developed, to other people, places, and dimensions or spheres (and eventually worlds) on the Tree of Life.

The energies of the Tree as they manifest in our aura appear in ideal archetypal form, but as they enter into the physical body, they shift, change, and express themselves in accordance with the needs of physical life, not spiritual. One need only recognize that the orbital pattern of the solar system is distinct and different from the stacked, linear hierarchy of powers presented on the Tree.

Just as the energies of the astral or watery World of Creation make their way into material existence through the planets and their etheric energies (creating the doctrines of astrology in the process), the same energies are manifested in the physical earth through mineral and plant life. The earth acts as a container for the total expression of all of the etheric and material energies of each of the individual planets. The human body also acts as a container for their same expression. This is first through the archetypes of the Tree in the aura, then by the psychic centers relating to the planets and elements in the etheric body, and finally through specific and distinct expression in the actual physical body and the organs related to those planets.

The planets derive their existence and energy from the spheres of the Tree of Life, but they are not identical. The energies of the planets are primarily material, etheric, and to some degree astral in nature, but they are not concerned with extremely abstract concepts or pure energy, as are the worlds of Briah and Atziluth, respectively.

For this reason, it is possible for someone to become a very powerful Kabbalist who is able to create seeming miracles in the material world, yet is not very developed in the spiritual sense. Through focusing on the relationship of the etheric energies of the planets, their interaction with the earth, and in turn our individual physical body and subconscious, profound and powerful energies can be released. This is the secret of practical alchemy and talismanic magic.

Genuine spiritual development requires that this be a stepping stone to further work aimed at Illumination and not an end in itself, in which case it would be little more than sorcery at best and genuine black magic at worst. The physical sciences are primarily concerned with the physical world of Assiah, from the cosmic origins expressed in the First Swirlings to the physical earth (Malkuth), its atomic substructure and the physical forces that created it and hold it together (the elements), and the physical human body (Guph). The etheric mesh or net (lower Nephesh) that allows all of this to take place is increasingly addressed in physics and other studies of subatomic matter. The Nephesh is also addressed in energetic healing modalities related to mind-body connections, such as alternative therapies (acupuncture, aromatherapy, therapeutic touch, hypnosis, homeopathy, and healing with magnets, crystals, and flower essences). The more personal aspects of the Nephesh, dealing with our personality and our subconscious and not the physical body, constitute the higher Nephesh (the Nephesh is one continuous stream, like the notes on a piano keyboard), and these energies are related to instinctual drives, urges, psychic ability, and paranormal phenomena.

The Nephesh is the key to all magical work. It is where the power is, and it is how we actually manifest in the material world. Without it, esotericism is little more than philosophic abstraction and academic research, degenerating into moralism, useless ideas, and bizarre fantasies, with the occasional experimentation into petty psychism.

The purpose of this scheme is to show that creation occurs through subtle changes in the levels of energy-matter, from the most subtle (fire) to the most dense (earth). Within this context of increasing density, there also arises a series of ten planes or levels of consciousness that combine with energy-matter, known as Sephiroth or spheres of being. They occur in a threefold pattern, three times—unity, polarity, synthesis—and finally the tenth is materialization. This basic idea of unity, polarity, and reharmonizing is the basis of Kabbalistic (and Hermetic) practices and is derived from the observation of Nature.

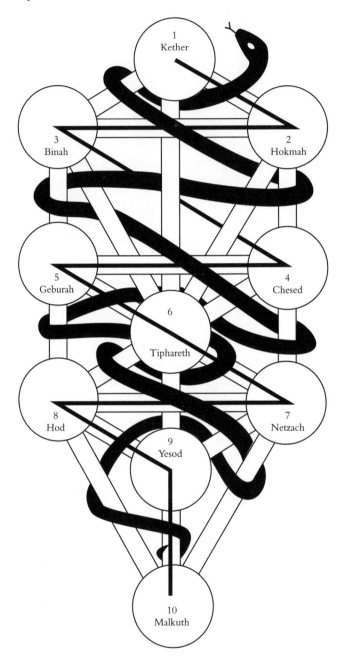

**The Path of the Serpent and the
Lightning Flash on the Tree of Life**

Each world is a reflection to a denser or subtler degree of the one before or after it. Each sphere (Sephirah[4]) is a reflection, in part, of what precedes or follows it. However, since each reflection is only partial, or slightly distorted, each sphere takes on its own unique characteristics. *Sephirah* can be translated as "sphere," "emanation," or "number," and its root, *seph,* is used in forming the word for "book." For this reason, the ten levels of the Tree of Life can also be visualized as round, luminous spheres of energy-consciousness-matter, each with its own characteristic that is related but not identical to those spheres which follow or which came before it.

This zigzag of creation is called *Mezla* and is also referred to as the "Lightning Flash." The return of energy from matter back through the various stages, spheres, and Worlds of Creation is known as the "Path of the Serpent," because of its reverse, or complementary, zigzag nature back up this diagram called the Tree of Life. It is also called the "Path of Return."

The Ten Levels of Creation

The goal of the mystic is to experience union with the Divine. This is an act of repair or healing that brings our entire being into fullness. The methods used are performed alone, or in a small group in the same way we would do them for ourselves. However, before we undertake a journey, particularly a journey within, it is important to have a map to guide us. For Kabbalists, this map is the Tree of Life.

The ten spheres of the cosmos emanating from the undifferentiated source, or Limitless Light (Ain Soph Aur), are as follows. Note that each sphere has a set of ideas associated with it, as well as a location in our psychic body that allows us to access those ideas and energy on a personal level. This energy is generally related to an area of the body, and is a good place to start, but it is not limited to that location and has other, more direct means of affecting the physical structure. According to traditional Kabbalistic teachings, the spheres came into existence when the divine names associated with them were each spoken by God. These names are particularly useful for attuning ourselves to the energy of each sphere. Most Hermetic schools use a set of names, consisting of a divine,

---

4 *Sephirah* is singular; *Sephiroth* is plural.

archangelic, angelic, and mundane name for each sphere. However, it is common to just use the divine name in Jewish schools—and also when first learning to use the pattern of the Tree in a practical manner.

The Crown (Kether) is unity. Kether contains all that potentially will be and all that has been. It is the Godhead and the font of creation.

Location: Top of head, brain as a whole.

Divine Name: Ehieh, pronounced "Eh-he-yeh," translated as "I Am"; also, Ehieh Asher Ehieh, or "I Am That I Am," but more accurately, "I Am That Which Is Becoming." Here, everything exists only in seed idea and potential, without form or individualized essence.

Wisdom (Hokmah) is thinking: a clear concept of what is, and the proper relationship between all of the aspects involved.

Location: Left side of the brain, temple.

Divine Name: YHVH, pronounced "Yod-Heh-Vau-Heh," translated as "God." Since this is considered the "Unpronounceable Name of God," only the first two letters are often used, pronounced as "Yah." From this, we also hear it said as "Yah-weh" and "Yah-ho-vah." *Yah*, or YH, is the seed power of God from which everything else flows. YHVH is the united power from which the Four Worlds, four elements, and four levels of the soul are created. Individualized essence exists, but only latently; it is yet to manifest.

Understanding (Binah) is the ability to know, as symbolized by Wisdom, but also to act, and the courage to do so. It is stability, focus, and power.

Location: Right side of the brain, temple.

Divine Name: YHVH Elohim, pronounced as "YHVH Ale-oh-heem," translated as "The Lord God." This refers to the creative energies being arranged and directed in a productive manner so that they can be available for use. It is the first manifestation of individuality on the most basic level.

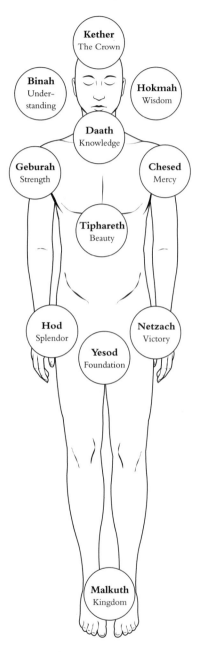

The Tree of Life in the Human Body

Knowledge (Daath) is an arising of awareness within oneself, the experience of moving from the theoretic to the practical, from the abstract to the concrete. Technically, Daath is not a sphere on the Tree of Life but an expression of greater synthesis of consciousness. Daath is not used directly in most Kabbalistic work, in that it naturally arises when new states of consciousness are permanently integrated. This integration appears to have an affinity with our nervous systems, and for that reason, Daath is attributed to either the throat (Adam's apple, appropriately) or the brainstem (medulla oblongata).

Mercy (Chesed) is compassion, but more importantly purity. Mercy provides us with the energy to be in the world but not of it, to be a morally and ethically upright—but not uptight—person. Mercy connects heaven and earth, and in its influence the divine plan is understood and expressed. Selflessness is the current manifest here. Just as the energies exist in potential in Kether, are formulated in Hokmah, and are made available in Binah, it is in Chesed that they are actually put into play.

Location: Left shoulder.

Divine Name: El, pronounced as "Ale" or "Ehl," translated as "God." It refers to the notion that "God is in His heaven and all is right with the world."

Strength (Geburah) is power, but more importantly, self-discipline. This is the ability to get to work on what needs to be done, and the courage to follow through. Here we mean the work of self-actualization, as well as the work of quieting the mind and getting down to business.

Location: Right shoulder.

Divine Name: Elohim Gibor, pronounced "Ale-oh-heem Gibor," translated as "Gods of Power" or "The Strength of God." This refers to the single-pointed focus that is required to achieve any activity of lasting value.

Beauty (Tiphareth) is the experience of "self" or "I." Here, we exist as an independent being but also feel the subtle and not-so-subtle connections to others and, more importantly, to our divine origins. This experience offers us the highest levels of subjectivity, or "selfness." The higher we go on the Tree, the more selfless we become, and the clearer our perception of our self, others, and the universe is. As we go lower, we become more selfish and marred in our perspective of people, things, and experiences.

Location: Heart and solar plexus.

Divine Name: YHVH Eloh va-ha-Daath, pronounced "YHVH El-oh-ah vah-Dah-ath." Some older systems simply use "Eloha," and some modern schools use the Gnostic name IAO, pronounced "Ee-Ah-Oh." Translated as "Lord God of Knowledge," or often "Knowledge of the Lord God," this refers to our direct experience of our inner spiritual nature, although this is still somewhat colored by our personal interpretations. It is our inner sense of Beingness as we progress on the Path of Return.

Victory (Netzach) is the interface between self and the material world. It is the domain of the emotions and, more importantly, of the instincts to be, have, and do.

Location: Left hip.

Divine Name: YHVH Tzabaoth, pronounced as "YHVH Tzah-bah-oth," translated as "Lord of Armies" (referring to the array of natural energies in creation).

Splendor (Hod) is the intellect, but also the highest level of human reason that if turned inward, can help us sense our connectedness to the Divine.

Location: Right hip.

Divine Name: Elohim Tzabaoth, pronounced as "Ale-oh-heem Tzah-bah-oth," translated as "God of Hosts" or "God of Armies" (referring to the array of mental power linking creation).

Foundation (Yesod) is the realm of the psyche, or soul, in the sea of creation, with all of its many parts, images, dreams, and aspirations. It is the power of the Godhead driving downward to create the material world, and also the pull of the Godhead on each of us to go inward, upward, and back to oneness with the Being of all. It is the basis for all creation and experiences in the material and psychic realms.

Location: Sexual organs.

Divine Name: Schaddi El Chai, pronounced as "Shah–dye Ale
   Kye," translated as "Almighty Living God."

Kingdom (Malkuth) is sovereignty and is the place of action, our body, and the material world. Kingdom is the strong pull of emotional desire (Victory) in action, in and around us—through our flesh and in the experiences of daily living. These powerful desires can be used to link us even deeper into material life, to link us to the Divine, or to a host of psychic subtleties between the two.

Location: Feet, but also the perineum when seated on the ground,
   or the organs of excretion (bowels).

Divine Name: Adoni ha-Aretz, pronounced "Ah-doh-ni ha-Ar-ets."
   This translates as "Lord of the Earth" but conceptually is our
   personal realization of God. When we pray, meditate, or ask for
   inspiration, it is to Adoni—our personal Lord—that we pray. It
   is our understanding of God that creates our own inner law or
   synthesis and thereby colors our expression of Divinity in daily
   life, or on earth.

Each of the spheres acts a kind of rest station as well as a focal point along the way. They are in turn connected to each other by a series of paths, which helps us to take the concepts they individually represent and combine them with each other in a systematic synthesis. There are ten Sephiroth and twenty-two paths.[5] It is through meditation on the different levels of the Tree of Life, and the paths that unite them, that we sharpen our awareness, increase our expression of divine potential, and bring healing to our body and mind.

---

5 These are often called, in total, the thirty-two Paths of Wisdom. Location and associations of the paths are
   fairly standardized, but variations in the Tree of Life exist.

To summarize Kabbalistic theories on creation, we could say that the visible and invisible worlds are interrelated and are in fact various projections of one another. Focal points of energy concentration exist, and these have specific functions in modifying the way we experience and perceive the relationship between energy, matter, and consciousness. Links between these focal points create new expressions of energy-matter-consciousness, as they represent a synthesis of the different focal points involved. Health and wellness are an expression of a harmonious relationship between these psychic points of contact, and are a byproduct of inner harmony. If we restore the psychic world to harmony, the material world will automatically follow. We could say, simplistically, that creation is a giant hologram over which we have far more influence than is generally understood or believed. Through proper training, we human beings all have the potential to be an active creator within this holographic structure (even to the degree that our very thoughts materialize), thereby increasing our physical, emotional, and mental wholeness.

Everybody Is a Star

Paracelsus was the greatest healer, alchemist, and practical Kabbalist of his age. As a physician, he wrote extensively on health, the role of medicine, attitude, and the sympathetic relationship between the visible and invisible forces in the healing process. It would be easy to dismiss him as an archaic remnant of a bygone age were it not for his contributions to allopathic and homeopathic medicine, success at curing the "incurable," and his ability to synthesize alchemical and Kabbalistic information into volumes of practical techniques. Paracelsus's writings are still followed to this day (almost religiously by some) in circles where the Elixir of Life or the Philosopher's Stone are sought.

"The mysteries of the Great (Macrocosm) and Little World (microcosm) are distinguished only by the form in which they manifest themselves; for they are one thing, one being. Heaven and earth have been created out of nothingness, but they are composed of three things—mercurius, sulphur, and sal. . . . Just as the Great World is thus built upon the three primordial substances, so man—the Little World—was composed of the same substances."

Paracelsus

Paracelsus's above quote is equally applicable to both allopathic and homeopathic medicines, and it demonstrates their essential unity. If we simply remove the words "mercurius, sulphur, and sal" and replace them with "life force, consciousness, and body," we can easily understand what is being said. It is this fundamental premise—that the physical world and the human body are universes in miniature that reflect the energies of the larger invisible universe of cosmic energy—that allows any esoteric or energetic healing practice to succeed.

The preceding theory is often called the "Doctrine of Correspondences," which lists the relationships between material objects and immaterial ideas, emotions, and energies. In Kabbalistic healing, as in almost all traditional energy-based and herbal-mineral healing, this doctrine is utilized in some form.

The Tree of Life offers us the easiest way to apply this information. An additional description is given in the *Sepher Yetzirah* that works quite well. This will be of exceptional interest to students of Reiki and similar systems that utilize letter symbols to energize the psychic and physical bodies.

Sacred speech permeates the psycho-spiritual practices from antiquity to the present era. Judaism was no different in this regard, and it saw Hebrew as a sort of divine language. If the Jews were the "chosen people" to receive God's message, then of course God spoke to them in Hebrew. Later, Hebrew became elevated to a "divine" or "angelic" language by Kabbalists of all stripes who used Greek, Latin, or other languages in their daily lives but Hebrew in their esoteric practices. This specialization of Hebrew was no different than what had happened to other languages, Sanskrit being the prime example.

Rationalizations aside, Hebrew, like many ancient languages, offers a unique opportunity to tap into vast reserves of psychic power buried in the collective unconscious. This arises simply because for the majority of its users, it is utilized only for specialized practices. Another benefit is that it has sonorous qualities that modern languages lack. It is easily chanted in a special manner called *vibrating*. In this method, the sounds of names and words are pronounced so as to create a literal vibration in the person saying them. This can easily be practiced to the point that others in the room will feel it as well, even if it is done quietly or silently.

As abstract symbols, Hebrew names and words act as a visual version of a Zen *koan*. Their shapes suggest certain ideas, but these ideas are for the most part foreign to modern life. Since when written they are physical structures, painted or drawn, they are easily visualized and thereby give the mind something to focus on. They are sufficiently removed from our daily lives, which allows our subconscious to create a host of associations for them that might never come to us by using rational analysis alone. As part of the collective experience of Western civilization, Hebrew also offers us an opportunity to tap into our collective experiences and the spiritual concepts that have shaped millennia of our history.

Using Hebrew Letters

Each letter is seen as sacred—the means whereby creation was accomplished. To visualize, write, inscribe, or utter their sounds is an act of creation that utilizes the primordial and divine energies they express. Like the ancient Egyptian hieroglyphs they are based on, the Hebrew letters are viewed as living entities or beings in and of themselves.

In ancient Hebrew, there are three mother letters, seven double letters, and twelve single letters. This means that there are three letters that are seen as the source of all the others, seven letters that have a soft and a hard means of pronunciation, and twelve letters that have a single manner of pronunciation.

Their general correspondences are as follows:

Three Mother Letters
Aleph—Air, primordial unity of spirit, but also matter and energy

Mem—Water, the matrix of creation, particularly material form

Shin—Fire, divine energy in action, movement of mind and body, consciousness

Seven Double Letters
Beth—Wisdom/Folly

Gimel—Grace/Indignation

Daleth—Fertility/Solitude

Kaph—Life/Death

Peh—Power/Servitude

Resh—Peace/War

Tau—Riches/Poverty

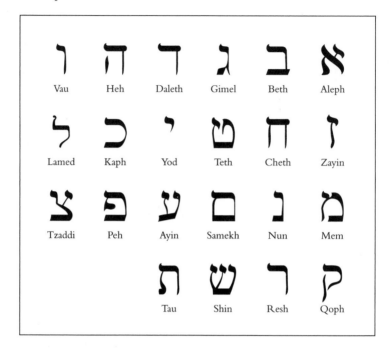

Each of the seven double letters also has a planetary relationship that is used in healing work.

Twelve Single Letters

Heh—Sight	**Lamed**—Work
Vau—Hearing	**Nun**—Movement
Zayin—Smell	**Samekh**—Anger
Cheth—Speech	**Ayin**—Mirth
Teth—Taste	**Tzaddi**—Imagination
Yod—Sexual love	**Qoph**—Sleep

As we can see, the letters can be used as focal points for meditation and prayer when working with specific life issues. This means that Heh can be used to strengthen our "vision" of spiritual and mental things, Teth can assist us in acquiring a "taste" for life, and Qoph can be used to induce sleep as well as to "awaken" us to ideas and feelings.

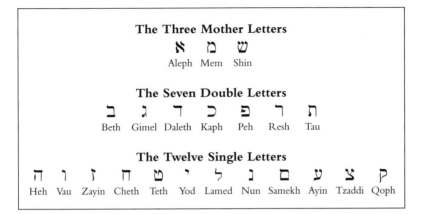

Finally, like the Sephiroth of the Tree of Life, each of the letters has a location in the psychic and physical body, making it a tangible access point for increasing desired qualities. As a whole, when applied in this manner, it refers to the archetypal being known as "Adam Kadmon," or the first human.

Astrological considerations can also come into play, as each of the single letters corresponds to a sign of the zodiac. This gives us a key to potential areas of weakness based on an astrological chart.

Adam Kadmon

Adam, or "Man," is interpreted as meaning all human beings, regardless of gender, but is specifically male in that it is active and outgoing in its energy. The Divine extended energy out from its center to create the universe, just as early men had to leave their homes to go and hunt for food. Adam Kadmon is the archetypal expression of this original state of being, which is personified in the story of Adam and Eve.

This Adam—a state of unified consciousness across creation that became an individualized being—is said to have "fallen" from a divine unit into pieces, similar to the myth of Osiris. This "fall" into matter effectively cut off any memory of its divine origins. This separation, while seen as a tragedy by many religious sects, is in fact a blessing. If it were not for the "fall" or descent of our consciousness into matter, we could never

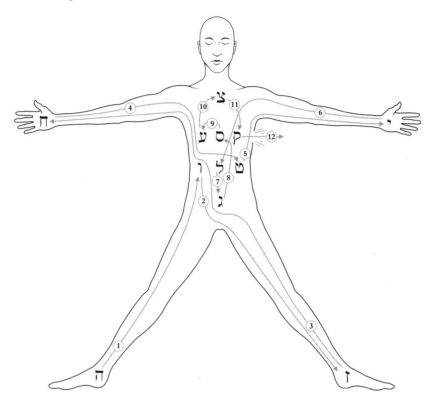

Path of the Energy of the Single Letters in Man's Body

have realized first our seeming separation from the Godhead, nor later our inherent oneness with it. In exercising free will, we grow as beings into fullness. This is important, as only by asking or allowing the mercy of the Divine to flow into our lives does it enter. We are masters of this kingdom, and it is up to us to allow in the rest of creation if we are to become whole. Students of shamanism will notice a similarity between this idea of the fall and the practice of soul retrieval, wherein the person is shattered and made whole through prayer, ritual, and meditation.

In Kabbalah, the easiest and most direct way to bring wholeness is through using correspondences, as they directly relate to the organ or area that is ill. They can be used as a starting point for psychological conditions as well, by using their astrological meaning. In Hebrew, like many ancient languages, speech and writing were considered sacred and magi-

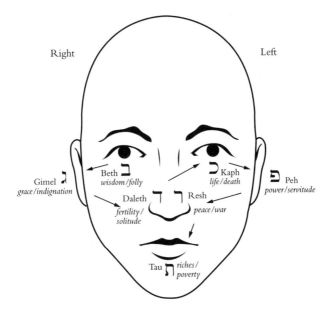

The Seven Double Letters in Man

cally powerful. Each Hebrew letter is seen as alive and filled with the power and intelligence that God created and used to make everything in creation. As such, humanity can use the letters to repair itself and to attune to the Divine. According to the *Sepher Yetzirah*, the Hebrew letters relate to the following areas of the human body:

Heh—Right foot	**Vau**—Right kidney	**Zayin**—Left foot
Cheth—Right hand	**Teth**—Left kidney	**Yod**—Left hand
Lamed—Bile	**Nun**—Intestines	**Samekh**—Stomach
Ayin—Liver	**Tzaddi**—Esophagus	**Qoph**—Spleen
Beth—Right eye	**Gimel**—Right ear	**Daleth**—Right nostril
Kaph—Left eye	**Peh**—Left ear	**Resh**—Left nostril
Tau—Mouth		

As for the three mother letters, Aleph is given to the chest, meaning the lungs and heart, as Aleph also symbolizes air, or the life force of creation. Shin is given to the head and represents the dynamic energy of consciousness, but also spiritual awakening, as Shin is also the mediator of the most abstract and powerful energies in Kabbalah. It is the dove that descended on Jesus and the tongues of flame at Pentecost. Mem is given to the stomach, and here represents assimilation and growth, but also the sexual organs and the womb, as it is the primordial waters of creation spoken of in Genesis and the waters of rebirth symbolized by Christian baptism.

Through the astrological and planetary correspondences of the letters, we have the entire rhythmic cycle of creation outlined, and we have directions on which days, as well as times of the year, specific energies are at their peak.

Exercise—Hebrew Letters and the Energy Body

Explanation—This exercise is to establish the Hebrew letters and their association with the psychic and physical body as a preliminary to using them for healing purposes or other advanced psychic practices.

Type of Practice—As needed, depending on the work one is undertaking.

Preparation—Relax as in previous exercises. Performance of the Ritual of Attunement to the Tradition or the Six Directions is optional.

Method—After preparations, proceed as follows:

1. Seated in a chair, or lying down, imagine that your body is luminous and empty of any solidity, filled with a brilliant light with a slightly bluish tinge. Focus your attention on your head and establish the Hebrew letter Shin in the center of it. Move down to your chest and establish the letter Aleph. Finally, move to your navel and establish the letter Mem.

2. Once the three mother letters are completed, move your attention to your right foot and imagine the letter Heh in the center of it, in brilliant white light.

3. After a minute or so, move your attention to your right kidney and visualize the letter Vau. Proceed then through the following chart, creating each of the Hebrew letters in their respective places.

4. After you are comfortable with the location of each letter and its formation in your imagination, proceed to associate the various properties or qualities that go with it. You may also begin to change the color of each letter to that listed,[6] or simply leave it as brilliant white. The properties are not to be associated with part of the body as a physical location, but rather with the Hebrew letter as their psychic expression. The physical location is a starting point for those properties and qualities, like a gate or door, and is not a destination.

5.

Letter	Location	Element	Color	Energy
Shin	Head/Brain	Fire	Red	Light
Aleph	Chest/Heart/Lungs	Air	Yellow	Life
Mem	Navel/Stomach	Water	Blue	Love

Letter	Organs of the Body	Astrological Sign	Color	Human Properties
Heh	Right foot	Aries	Red	Sight
Vau	Right kidney	Taurus	Red-orange	Hearing
Zayin	Left foot	Gemini	Orange	Smell
Cheth	Right hand	Cancer	Orange-yellow	Speech
Teth	Left kidney	Leo	Yellow	Taste
Yod	Left hand	Virgo	Yellow-green	Sexual love
Lamed	Bile	Libra	Green	Work
Nun	Intestines	Scorpio	Green-blue	Movement
Samekh	Stomach	Sagittarius	Blue	Anger
Ayin	Liver	Capricorn	Blue-violet (indigo)	Mirth
Tzaddi	Esophagus	Aquarius	Violet	Imagination
Qoph	Spleen	Pisces	Red-violet	Sleep

6 This color scale, taken from the Golden Dawn, is known as the King Scale and represents the letter-color relationship as it appears on the paths of the Tree of Life. Other color schemes exist and have been used successfully across the centuries.

Letter	Organs of the Head	Planetary Energy	Color	Double Qualities
Beth	Right eye	Moon	Yellow	Wisdom/Folly
Gimel	Right ear	Mars	Blue	Grace/Indignation
Daleth	Right nostril	Sun	Green	Fertility/Solitude
Kaph	Left eye	Venus	Violet	Life/Death
Peh	Left ear	Mercury	Red	Power/Servitude
Resh	Left nostril	Saturn	Orange	Peace/War
Tau	Mouth	Jupiter	Indigo	Riches/Poverty

Incorporation into Daily Practice—Practice this method daily for two weeks to become familiar with it, then as needed. After three or four sessions, this exercise is far easier than it first appears. Repeat it regularly during the two weeks prior to the full moon following the spring and fall equinoxes as a means of strengthening your psychic attunement to the energies the letters manifest.

Exercise—Using Hebrew Letters to Heal Another Person

Explanation—The psychic qualities of the Hebrew letters can be used to stimulate the astral body of another person, in the same manner that letters, images, and figures have been used for millennia. They can also be used as a starting point to emphasize particular healing energies in a person, whereby these energies spread out to a specific afflicted area or to the entire psychic and physical bodies.

Type of Practice—A healing technique to be used as needed.

Preparation—The practitioner and recipient should prepare through several minutes of deep breathing, relaxation, and either silent or verbal prayer. The recipient should be seated or lying flat on a couch, bed, or massage table so that the practitioner can work standing or seated next to the recipient as needed.

Method—After preparations are completed, proceed as follows:
1. With the problem to be treated clearly identified, visualize the formation of the Hebrew letters in the psychic body of the recipient.

Imagine that the body is empty of dense matter and is made of luminous energy and light. You can dispense with visualizations of interior organs if you do not know their exact position and appearance. If you do know their appearance and position, then they can also be visualized as very clear, bright, and luminous and in perfect form and function.

2. Form the letter Shin in the center of the recipient's head, the letter Aleph in the chest, and the letter Mem behind the navel.

3. Once completed, start with the letter Heh and imagine each of the letters in their proper locations, radiating clear and bright energy. The exact concept can be added later. In the beginning, simply focus on the letter radiating its energy, and bring the entire psychic body into harmony with its specific function, even if not remembered at the time.

4. Work your way through all of the letters, paying attention to any area where there is resistance, heaviness, or a sense of sluggishness. Go back to that area after you have completed implanting the energetic seed ideas that the letters represent into the psychic body of the recipient.

5. Once you have completed all of the letters, visualize the energy moving from Heh through Qoph freely, smoothly, and powerfully. Repeat with the organs of the head, starting with Beth and ending with Tau. (See diagrams on pages 72 and 73.)

6. Go back and focus your attention on any areas of resistance. Bring in more light, a sense of vitality, and love to the afflicted area.

7. When you are completed, imagine that brilliant white light is entering into the recipient's head at the crown and flooding the body with brilliant light, and that the letters are energized and in harmony with it.

8. Focus on the letter Shin and sense that it is bringing the energy of the invisible into the visible and the energy of the intangible into the tangible.

9. Move to the letter Aleph and sense that the body and mind are one, that energy and matter are one, and that as you will with your heart

and mind and the recipient wills with his or her heart and mind, all healing is done and accomplished.

10. Move to the letter Mem and imagine that the recipient's subconscious mind accepts this healing energy and that the recipient's etheric body works and manifests this healing energy into material form.

11. When completed, see the recipient's body bathed in luminous light and allow the recipient to rest for a few minutes. Ring a bell, clap your hands, or use a small gong to reintegrate him or her into waking consciousness.

Incorporation into Daily Practice—Use as needed in working with others.

Four Elements, Worlds, and Bodies

For physical health, we can use the Hebrew letters, or we can use them in connection with the Sephiroth, in relation to their connecting paths. This is called Pathworking. In addition to their above correspondences, the spheres also relate to the planets and, as such, act like psychic centers in us. They also have an elemental quality; that is, they have an affinity for one of the ancient elements of earth, water, air, or fire.

These elements have nothing to do with the material bodies of the same name, and as such are called "elemental" to distinguish them from the earth we walk on, the water we drink, the air we breathe, and the fire we cook with. They are, in fact, energetic states, each with their own unique characteristics, as well as each of the previously mentioned ten levels of consciousness within them. Earth represents solidity, water represents liquids, air represents gases, and fire represents pure energy.

From this simple construct, we can assist someone to get more "grounded" with earth, and we can direct the earth energy to their bones, teeth, and muscular system to repair injury. Water energy can be used to assist in reproduction, circulation, excretion, and digestion. Air can be used for respiration, as well as nerves and mental uneasiness. Fire invigorates and brings life and self-consciousness to the forefront. In more complex models of the Tree of Life, these elements are also attributed to the various worlds (*O'lam*) in which we exist. In modern energetic healing, this would relate to the theory of "four bodies": physical, emotional, mental, and spiritual. We say "body" because each aspect represented interrelates to the others, just as the Sephiroth do, and like them, each is a miniature representation of the whole. It is its own little universe, or world, but with a very distinct bias and function.

The energy of life or consciousness manifests in two forms: fire and air. While both are predominately active in nature, fire is the more active of the two, with air being slightly passive because of the partial water element in its makeup. Potential matter, both organic and inorganic, manifests its energy as water and earth.

There are, in fact, forty different ways that energy-matter-consciousness can manifest in our world. However, this level of complexity is rarely the concern of most Kabbalistic meditations or healing practices.

In the East, the idea of principal elements is expressed in more or less the same manner as in the West. In Indian philosophy, as well as in modern occult or New Age circles, this original undifferentiated energy from creation is often called *akasha*, or Spirit. However, akasha consists of two aspects, one active and the other passive. The active energies are also referred to as the force of *kundalini*, or "spiritual forces." In alchemy, this is the Secret Fire. To the passive energies belongs the force of vital energy.

The function of vital energy is to maintain physical life forms and existence. It is completely instinctual and unconscious and is heavily influenced by cosmic cycles, astrological pulses, and other natural phenomena. The function of the Secret Fire, an active energy, is to increase in humanity (the only place where it is present) its sense of self, or "I." At the lowest level of functioning, this is the ego; at the highest, it is Divinity incarnate, as both are two sides of the same coin. One is "self" in relation to the physical world and others; the other is "Self" in relationship to all of creation and as a co-creator.

In the vast majority of humanity, this Secret Fire, or liberating energy of self-consciousness, lies dormant, asleep at the base of the spine, coiled like a serpent. Only a small amount manages to escape, reaching a Sephirothic level, or so-called psychic center (chakra), thus creating a locus of consciousness for each person. If it reaches the top of the skull—and beyond—

a spiritual awakening can occur, allowing for a descent and re-ascent of the energy, during which the psychic centers can be awakened, opening the way for the manifestation of psychic powers and related phenomena.

As we can see, the concept of kundalini, or the Secret Fire, is linked to two polar concepts: first, that of the undifferentiated creative energy, and second, that the seed of this energy is locked on each cell of material creation and is focused in humanity at the base of the spine. If the energy becomes concentrated in the head, it can create the illusion of a spiritual awakening, in addition to causing the well-known "hot and cold" flashes, or currents, up and down the spine. When this energy rises as a result of psychic experiences, and not because of physical weakness, it can cause the body's vital energy to be concentrated on various areas of the body, which creates physical and psychic disturbances.

These physical and psychic disturbances are a result of the detoxification of that part of the psychic body closest to the physical body. In energetic healing, this is often referred to as the etheric body. In Kabbalah, it is known as the Nephesh, and the physical body called the Guph.

All physical healing requires that the energies of the etheric body, or Nephesh, be reharmonized. In fact, physical healing requires that the etheric body of the healer be strong as well, as some of the healer's energy is used to create a bridge between him or herself and the recipient in most cases (and in all cases in which physical contact is used). When distance healing is performed, it is the energies of the higher consciousness that are utilized.

The Four Souls of Being

Among the most confusing, abused, and misunderstood words in the Scriptures for many people is the word *soul*. In Kabbalah, there is the doctrine that each person has four souls. If we look carefully at how this word is used, it becomes clear that what is being said is that each person has four major areas of consciousness. In Christian circles, we often hear of someone "losing his immortal soul," and we wonder what that means. If we interpret the statement according to Kabbalah, we read it as "losing

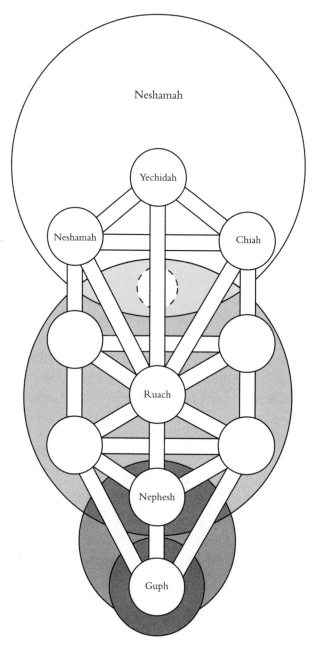

The Divisions of the Soul

his immortal consciousness," or, essentially, the awareness of his divine nature.

What is also unique in Kabbalah is that the physical body is given its own soul or consciousness. We can clearly see this each day as the body acts in manners we are completely unaware of—digestion, respiration, circulation, repair and destruction of cells, and combating disease, for instance.

Then there is the instinctual soul, or the unconscious forces that drive us to eat, sleep, have sex, practice fight or flight, and so on. We may be unaware of these forces, but they significantly determine how we interact with others and view the universe. This is called the Nephesh, which, as we have seen, also affects our material body in a direct manner. For this reason, some schools of Kabbalah only refer to the Nephesh and not the Guph, but you should know both that they are intimately linked and that, with very rare exceptions, they separate only at death.

Thirdly, there is the Ruach, or rational soul, which is the consciousness most people are aware of on a daily basis. This is composed of several parts and is illustrated by the five spheres of Chesed through Hod, with Tiphareth being the focal point of the Ruach on the Tree of Life, just as Yesod is the focal point of the Nephesh and Malkuth the focal point of the Guph.

Finally, there is the Neshamah, or spiritual consciousness, which is composed of three subdivisions, or the top three spheres of the Tree. This is our immortal consciousness and its functions of Being (Kether), Divine Will or impulse to Become (Hokmah), and Intuition (Binah), which is the Voice of God speaking to us.

This final model of the overlap of Kabbalistic physiology and psychology can be confusing at first, and it is not essential that you understand the details. Simply come back to it every now and then and seek to understand it and synthesize it into your practice. It is sufficient to know that we are complex, multileveled beings. Yet simple and direct meditations and prayers can bring astounding results, peace of mind, and harmony to our consciousness on all levels.

A simple and functional model is to look at it as such:

Physical body and consciousness—Earth	Focused in Malkuth	Feet/Perineum
Emotional consciousness—Water	Focused in Yesod	Sexual organs
Intellectual consciousness/Ego—Fire	Focused in Tiphareth	Heart/Solar plexus*
Link between ego and self—Air	Focused in Daath	Throat**
Immortal consciousness—Spirit	Focused in Kether	Crown

* The exact location varies from author to author, the most common being (1) the area of the physical heart, (2) slightly below the sternum, (3) the solar plexus (stomach), and (4) the solar plexus (navel).

** This should really be the medulla oblongata, as that is the seat of unconscious bodily and psychic functioning. In her work *The Circuit of Force*, Dion Fortune eventually changed her attribution of Daath to this area of the brain, but the original location still holds in most written works. A point midway between the two could be used as well, as long as it is strongly energizing the brain stem and the surrounding area. See also: Mark Stavish, "Secret Fire: The Relationship Between Kundalini, Qabala, and Alchemy" (1997), www.hermetic.com/stavish/essays/secret-fire.html.

The etheric or intermediary consciousness between the physical and emotional domains, while not listed, can be thought of as firmly linking these two "bodies."

By linking these types of consciousness to their primary focal points in the Tree of Life, we will have a practical tool for when we work directly on the psychic centers within the body. This is particularly true for students familiar with the exercise known as the "Middle Pillar," a form of Kabbalistic kundalini yoga that awakens the centers, brings them into action and harmony with each other, and brings health and well-being to the total person. The physical focal points will be explained in detail in chapters 6 and 7.

The Middle Pillar Exercise is well known and is easily located in printed and electronic sources, mostly authored by Israel Regardie. What becomes immediately clear is that Regardie developed at least four different versions of the Middle Pillar over his magical career. The earliest of these versions was what he received from his training in the Stella Matutina and modified as a preliminary exercise to what he published in *The Art of True Healing*. This book became the basis for his later work in *The Middle Pillar*, with a third variation appearing in *The Meaning of Magic*. A fourth version, appearing as "The Royal Ritual of the Middle Pillar," includes Enochian and a vast array of angelic forces as part of the invocation.[7] The most significant difference between these various versions is that some use the elements and some use the spheres of the Tree of Life as they appear on the Middle Pillar.[8] All are effective; however, in order to maintain a coherent and congruent subconscious synthesis of the ideas we are seeking to practically apply, we will use the spheres only for expanding states of consciousness, while using the elements to expand our available energy. This is easily understood when we remember that the elements are unconscious instinctual etheric forces that create, bind, and dissolve the material universe. They are active in us, but we are mostly unconscious of them; as such, their true power is more latent than active. By directly addressing them, we bring them into full awareness and manifestation.[9]

Exercise—The Middle Pillar of the Elements

Explanation—In the practice of the Six Directions, the elements are invoked around us to assist us in establishing our place in time and space as well as to give us a sense of the invisible energies that create the visible world. In this version of the Middle Pillar, we internalize these same energies, using the same divine names, colors, and symbols, by linking them to specific psychic clusters in our etheric and physical bodies. Here, we begin to understand that the Hermetic axiom is not just "As above, so below," but also, "As within, so without."

Type of Practice—Core practice.

Preparation—Prepare as previously directed. Sit, relax, breathe deeply, and if time allows perform the purification practice, followed by the Six Directions and the Attunement to the Tradition. The Middle Pillar should

---

7 Israel Regardie, "The Royal Ritual of the Middle Pillar," ed. Sir David Cherubim, Israel Regardie Foundation (1990), http://www.acc.umu.se/~stradh/magick/Rituals/Middle_pillar/regardie_ritual. The entire ritual is two pages in length.

8 For experienced students of Kabbalah and those familiar with the Golden Dawn system, the following rubric should be followed: When using the Middle Pillar as part of, or to build, the Tree of Life complete in one's aura, use the divine names of the Sephiroth. When using the Middle Pillar to awaken and direct the etheric energies of the physical world and the Nephesh, use the elemental names as they are given here. When using the Middle Pillar to strengthen the flow of energy from the spheres into the unconscious-etheric structure, use the great names as they are given in various Golden Dawn sources.

9 For a full discussion of the various forms of the Middle Pillar, see: Mark Stavish, "Secret Fire: The Relationship Between Kundalini, Kabbalah, and Alchemy" (1997), www.hermetic.com/stavish/essays/secret -fire.html.

initially be performed standing to allow for a clear formation of the "Pillar." Once you gain experience, you can do it seated (even seated on the ground) or kneeling in classical prayer and meditation postures.

Method—After preparation is complete, begin as follows:

1. Imagine a brilliant sphere of white light above your head. Its center is so bright that it appears like a black dot. The center point should be small, like a marble at most, from which the rest of the sphere is sensed as a radiation of light and energy with a clear, firm surface. This is the indwelling spirit of Divinity; it is the realm of Spirit (unity), and from it all things come. Vibrate the divine name Ehieh (pronounced "Eh-heh-yeh"). Dwell in this sphere for a few minutes and then proceed to visualize a shaft of brilliant light to the region of the throat.

2. At the throat, behind the Adam's apple and slightly toward the neck, imagine a small yellow sphere with violet highlights on the edges that is the size of a marble. It radiates a field of energy that forms a sphere about the size of a basketball, extending from roughly the bridge of the nose to above the heart. This is the air center, and it is the organizing energies of Being. Sense the presence of air. From it comes the power of the spoken word to create materially and spiritually. Enter into this center, experience its radiant energy, and then vibrate the divine name YHVH (pronounced "Yah-weh" or "Yah-ho-vah"). Stay with this feeling for a while and then extend the shaft of brilliant light to the solar plexus, halfway between the sternum and the navel (sometimes slightly higher, toward the sternum).

3. At the solar plexus is the fire center. This is the expression of our emotional energy in action, our power of love to transform all situations and conditions. Here, a small red point with green highlights on the edges forms and radiates a sphere of brilliant, hot, fiery energy. Stabilize this energy center and vibrate its divine name, Elohim (pronounced "Ale-oh-heem"). Rest in this center for a while and then extend the shaft of light to the pubic bone.

4. At the pubic bone is the center point of the water center. This is our creative energies, psychic potential, and instinctual energies of the

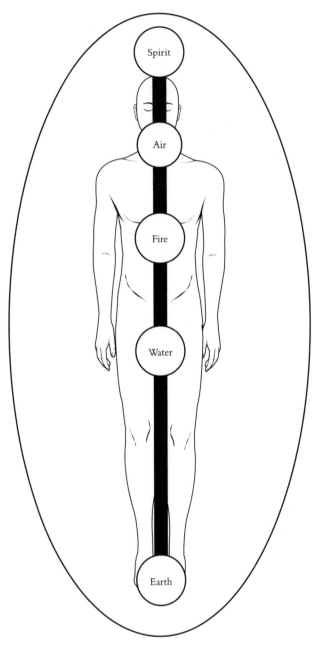

The Middle Pillar

subconscious. Here is a small blue sphere with orange highlights on the edges, and it creates another sphere about the size of a basketball. Stabilize the sphere and vibrate the divine name El (pronounced "Ale"). Rest in this sphere for a while and then extend the shaft of light to below your feet. Feel it uniting with the fiery energies at the center of the earth.

5. Next, imagine a small sphere of brilliant brick-red (russet) light forming a larger sphere of energy around it, and imagine this as if you were standing not on top of a basketball or soccer ball but with your feet about one-third inside of it. A dark, rich green is also often used so that the colors are in harmony with those being used for the elements elsewhere. This is the earth center, and it is the physical expression in form and action of the other spheres combined. This is our blessing upon all that is, was, and can be. Vibrate the divine name Adoni (pronounced "Ah-doh-ni").

6. Pause and establish these five brilliant colored spheres as connected by a shaft of brilliant light inside your empty, luminous body.

7. Focus your attention at the Spirit center above your head. As you breathe in, imagine a shaft or wave of light move from the center down your left side and into the earth. Hold your breath for a few seconds and then exhale, and as you do, imagine this light moving through your feet and up your right side, back to the Spirit center. Perform this three or seven times.

8. Focus your attention in your Spirit center, and as you inhale, imagine a shaft or wave of light moving down your front to merge with the earth center. Hold your breath, and as you exhale, imagine it moving up your back and merging with the Spirit center. Perform this three or seven times.

9. Inhale, and pull light down the center column from which the spheres radiate their light and energy. Feel it merge with the earth. As you exhale, imagine it rushing upward, stimulating the centers and merging them into one another on its way into the Spirit center. Feel the energy spray out the top of your head, through the Spirit center, and

rain down along the surface of your extended aura, smoothing out any roughness or imperfections and collecting at the earth center. Repeat this three or seven times.

10. Inhale, pulling the energy down the central column, and hold the energy at the earth center. When you exhale, imagine your body being wrapped in overlaying swaths of light, like a mummy, that turn one over the other from left and right until they reach the Spirit center. If you are seated or standing, you may cross your arms over your chest to make the visualization easier.

11. Breathe down a final ray of light from the Spirit center, and see it reach the earth. Feel the connection between your earth center and the physical-etheric earth. Exhale and see brilliant rays of the Secret Fire move up through your water center and merge with your fire center. Feel the fire center radiate life, energy, and light to all parts of your radiant hallowed body and then outward to the edges of your aura itself. You may at this point intone the divine name Amen (pronounced "Ah-mehn"), meaning, "So be it! It is Done!" This new vibration will seal your aura.

12. When you have completed the exercise, drop your hands and proceed with your meditation of the day or scheduled healing practice.

Incorporation into Daily Practice—The Middle Pillar can be performed daily prior to meditation, with or without the practice of the Six Directions. If this is not possible, perform it every other day, alternating with another exercise. If possible, perform the Six Directions, the Attunement to the Tradition, and the Middle Pillar as a complete practice at least once a week.

As you develop experience with the Middle Pillar, begin placing the elemental and Kerubic signs inside of each sphere. Also, make the center point of each sphere, where these symbols are located, small, about the size of a grain of rice, but remember that their influence is powerful enough to create the entire sphere or center. It is important during each and every practice session to place yourself in the center of each sphere and to experience it, even if for a second, as if it were an entire world.

This adds tremendous focus and power to each of the psychic clusters you are developing, rather than simply imagining them as large colored balls or lights.

An Important Note

Kabbalistic healing is very dynamic and resilient. Any one of the models presented can be used alone or in synthesis with the others. Simply pick a model and begin the process of integrating it into your own psyche. Move on to another model, and finally a third. Take careful notes of your experiences and synthesize them as you proceed. Remember, each of these models developed at a specific time and place in history. Over time, they were slowly brought together to be used by Kabbalists as a single system. Still, each is complete in itself and can be used and understood as a self-standing entity. Don't worry about being wrong or making mistakes. Simply follow the directions given in this and other recommended books, and enjoy your personal discovery of *your inner energies* and their effect on your physical health and experiences through Kabbalah.

On the surface, it seems like a lot of information, but practice makes it easy and reveals more to the student than books can say.

Exercise—Using the Middle Pillar in Healing Practices

Explanation—The Middle Pillar Exercise established vital psychic centers and connections in our aura and etheric body, using the physical body as a touchstone. Through sympathetic resonance, we can assist others in establishing these connections, as we establish them within ourselves, using contact and proximity to assist us.

Type of Practice—Core practice for healing purposes.

Preparation—The practitioner and recipient should prepare through several minutes of deep breathing, relaxation, and either silent or verbal prayer. The easiest way to utilize the Middle Pillar in healing is for the practitioner to be standing behind the recipient, hands on the recipient's shoulders, close to the neck and spine. The exercise can also be done seated beside the recipient. In this instance, Regardie suggests that the recipient sit with the legs crossed over the ankles, hands clasped at the solar plexus. The practitioner sits on the recipient's dominant side and places the corresponding hand under the recipient's clasped hands, and the remaining hand on the recipient's forehead. The recipient must be passive, receptive, and optimistic about the possible outcome of the session.

Method—After you and the recipient are ready, proceed as follows:

1. Perform the Middle Pillar, vocalizing the divine names and visualizing the psychic center and its element.

2. After each psychic center and its element is visualized, imagine its corresponding psychic center in the recipient being established and dynamically present.

3. Circulate the light as previously directed, focusing only on your performance of the Middle Pillar. Do not force the energy to flow in the recipient; only suggest or briefly imagine that it does, and return to your performance of the technique. Through physical contact and psychic suggestion, the energy flows in the recipient automatically.

4. When completed, simply break the physical connection and sit quietly for a moment or two. Ring a bell or clap loudly so that both parties reintegrate into the present moment.

Incorporation into Daily Practice—The Middle Pillar can form the core of a healing practice, particularly if assisting in the healing of others, when performed on a daily basis or more than once a week.

The Flashing Sword

The technique of the "Flashing Sword" is among one of the most common methods known to Kabbalists, and yet it is the least commented on. Like many esoteric practices, it lends itself to a great deal of sophistication. It can be introduced to beginning students as a practical mnemonic device for learning the basics of the Tree of Life, and it can become a method for releasing the Secret Fire.

The Flashing Sword represents the original descent of divine energy, or *Mezla,* during the act of creation. Once this act was accomplished, the energy began to rise again toward its original source. This became known to Kabbalists as the "Rising Serpent," also known as the Path of Return. Together, they form a symbolic glyph of the entire creative process and are well known to Hermetic students (see diagram on page 60).

When this process of creation is imagined as part of ourselves, we take on the role of creator and created. The Lightning Flash of creation goes through us, and we become re-created on a subtle and interior level. When this energy returns to its source, we are lifted ever so slightly higher on the Path of Return. Our psychic centers, corresponding to the spheres on the Tree, are awakened and brought into harmony with each other. We become the Adam Kadmon, or original human before the so-called fall. In short, since we are in our daily life already "fallen," by performing this and other esoteric exercises, we take on the role of redeemer of ourselves and creation.

Exercise—The Flashing Sword of Mezla

Explanation—This practice establishes the various spheres of the Tree of Life as a living potency in the aura of the practitioner, thereby making the intelligence and energy represented by those spheres more readily available to the practitioner. This can also assist in opening up to the various levels above the material world, so that interior initiation may occur.

Type of Practice—Core practice.

Preparation—The Attunement to the Tradition and/or the Six Directions should be performed prior to the Flashing Sword whenever possible.

Version One

Method—Once the preparations are completed, proceed as follows:
  1. Visualize your body as clear, hollow, and sparkling, like a crystal or diamond. Visualize a sphere of light above your head. Make it so intense that its center point appears black. Concentrate on this sphere

for several minutes. Watch it pulse and grow brighter, hotter, and more intense with each breath.

2. Imagine a ray of light coming down from it and piercing the top of your head, or the crown area, where the skull bones come together. Feel the ray enter into the center of your head, filling it with brilliant, intense light.

3. Feel a ray of this light move over to the left temple, filling the entire left side of your skull, brain, and face with light.

4. After a minute or two, imagine the ray of light moving over to the right temple, filling it with light. Meditate on this for a minute or two. Pause now, and visualize these three brilliant spheres of light—the crown, left temple, and right temple—connected by three rays of light from their center points, forming a triangle with a brilliant point of light in the center. Let this grow and fuse into a single sphere of brilliant light.

5. Let a ray of light now pass down from your right side to your left shoulder.

6. After a minute or so, let the ray continue toward your right shoulder.

7. Then the ray moves to your heart area, below the sternum, forming a brilliant sphere of clear, diamond-like light.

8. After a minute or so, the light extends to your left hip, forming a sphere there.

9. The ray continues across to your right hip, forming an additional sphere.

10. After a minute or so, the light extends to your pubic bone, forming a sphere.

11. The light continues to the center of your feet, as if you were standing in a brilliant ball of light. (If you are seated on the ground, use your perineum.) You can also imagine the energy continuing to the fiery center of the earth.

12. Pause and imagine this brilliant, flashing zigzag of light connecting the ten spheres of the Tree of Life inside your clear, brilliant, light-radiating body. Each sphere should be brilliant, bright, warm, and vi-

brant. The lines connecting them should be a brilliant bluish-white color and have sharp, clear edges.

You may end your meditation at this point. If you feel the energy is too intense or feel a sense of drowsiness or heaviness, withdraw the point of light from your feet and reverse the light, taking the spheres with you back to Kether, to the starting point above your head. Let that light then fade to black.

Incorporation into Daily Practice—This should be done at least once daily for two weeks to become familiar with the spheres and their locations. Afterward, it can be reduced to once a week and then once per month—but no less than four times a year, on the equinoxes and solstices.

Version Two

Method—Proceed as follows:

1. Perform the same as in Version One.

2. After reaching Malkuth at your feet, imagine a brilliant green serpent with red-gold highlights, accompanied by an intense sense of heat, rising up through each sphere and taking the energy of each sphere with it all the way to Kether.

3. Visualize the serpent's hood fanning out like a cobra's, overshadowing you in its power, protection, and wisdom.

4. Imagine both the downward flow of Mezla, the sword of light, and the upward power of the serpent combined. Hold this image and then rest in the feelings it creates, letting the actual image fade away. If the energy is too intense, reverse the serpent back to Malkuth and then the sword back to Kether.

Incorporation into Daily Practice—Same as in Version One.

Version Three

In this version, the entire Tree of Life is formulated in the aura, and the divine names previously discussed are used to energize the spheres and bring them into harmony with each other. In addition, a color of each

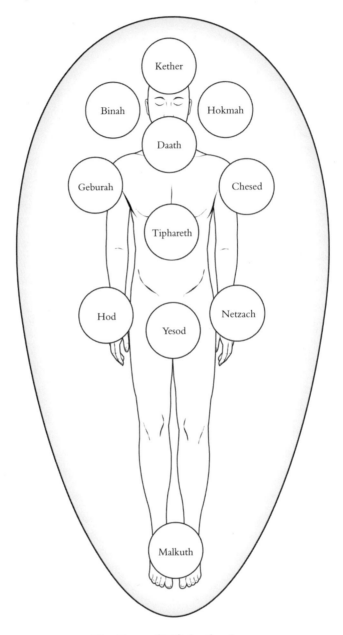

The Tree of Life in the Aura

sphere is used to bring greater focus to the entire exercise. Vibrate the divine name for each sphere, meditate on absorbing the energy of the sphere for a minute or two, and then move on to the next.

For example, imagine the sphere of Kether above your head. Feel its energy pulsing strongly from its center. Place yourself in the center of the sphere and sing the divine name associated with Kether—placing emphasis on the vowels—as if you were chanting the name.

It is a good idea to practice the sounds by focusing your attention on your solar plexus. When you have the right sound and pitch, you will feel a distinct sensation there. Once achieved, you can then get the same sensation when you are focusing on the sphere and vibrating the names, regardless of where the sphere is located. Your solar plexus acts as a tuning fork and helps you tune in to the right vibration.

The more you work and the less you read, the more you will get out of magic and the more effective your healing practice will become.

Sphere	Location	Color	Divine Name
Kether	Crown	Brilliant white	Ehieh
Hokmah	Left temple	Pearl gray	YHVH
Binah	Right temple	Black	YHVH Elohim
Chesed	Left shoulder	Blue	El
Geburah	Right shoulder	Scarlet red	Elohim Gibor
Tiphareth	Heart or solar plexus	Gold	Eloha va ha-Daath
Netzach	Left hip	Emerald green	YHVH Tzabaoth
Hod	Right hip	Orange	Elohim Tzabaoth
Yesod	Pubic bone	Purple	Schaddi El Chai
Malkuth	Soles of feet	Black, citron, olive, russet	Adoni ha-Aretz

Exercise—Using the Flashing Sword in Healing Practices

Explanation—This practice is to help awaken and stimulate the Tree of Life in the recipient's aura, as a preliminary to psychic healing, spiritual study, or even initiation.

Type of Practice—Healing technique.

Preparation—The practitioner and recipient should prepare through several minutes of deep breathing, relaxation, and either silent or verbal prayer.

Method—After the initial preparation, proceed as follows:

1. Standing behind the recipient with your hands on the recipient's neck, thumbs touching the spinal cord if possible, begin to formulate the Tree of Life in your own aura.

2. After each sphere is formed, imagine the same sphere as forming in the aura of the recipient.

3. If you are using divine names, they vibrate both your sphere and the sphere of the recipient simultaneously.

4. The entire Tree of Life is created in this mirror fashion.

5. Once you reach Malkuth, both you and the recipient will rest in the energy brought into play and allow it to permeate your bodies. You can mentally suggest that this energy cleanse the recipient of all mental, emotional, and physical obstructions to health and that the recipient is returned to a state of harmony and wellness.

Incorporation into Daily Practice—This can be utilized daily or as needed, depending on the particular discretion of the practitioner and recipient's needs.

As you achieve proficiency in the techniques, the following colors should be used for each sphere.

Sphere	Color
Kether	Brilliant white
Hokmah	Pearl gray
Binah	Shining black
Chesed	Azure blue
Geburah	Scarlet red
Tiphareth	Golden yellow
Netzach	Emerald green
Hod	Orange
Yesod	Violet-purple
Malkuth	Can be imagined as a single sphere of rich, dark brick red

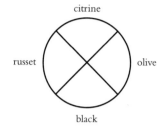

Malkuth is usually imagined as a circle divided into four quarters, with the uppermost quarter being citrine (yellow-green) in color, the bottom quarter black, the *operator's* right-hand quarter russet (dark red), and the left-hand quarter olive (the color of ripe olives, or a dark purple-black). Since each quarter represents one of the four elements of air (upper), earth (lower), fire (right), and water (left), the colors of yellow, dark green, red, and blue can also be used, thereby tying the practice into the Six Directions and the elemental Middle Pillar.

Key Points

- The *Sepher Yetzirah*, or Book of Formation, is a key Kabbalistic text.
- The Tree of Life, and its ten levels, is the main tool in modern Kabbalah for explaining the universe and our place in it.
- Hebrew letters are attributed specific powers or energies and relationships to the times of the year and organs in the human body.
- There are four distinct levels of consciousness, or the soul, in Kabbalah. Consciously harmonizing these levels brings health, wisdom, and happiness.
- The Guph is the physical body, the lower Nephesh is the etheric body, the higher Nephesh is the astral body, the Ruach is our sense of self or ego, and the Neshamah is our seed consciousness from which all the previous levels of consciousness and form grow.
- The Middle Pillar Exercise is fundamental to developing experience and control over the etheric and psychic elements that create our psychic, etheric, and material bodies.

- The Flashing Sword Exercise makes our understanding of the Tree of Life experiential by relating it to areas of the physical body. By building the Tree of Life in our aura, we create a conduit for its energies to more easily enter our psychic, etheric, and physical bodies.

Assignments for Chapter 3

1. Integrate the Middle Pillar Exercise into your practice schedule, performing it at least twice a week. Increase the amount of sessions spent with the Middle Pillar to once daily by the end of three months.

2. Integrate the Flashing Sword into your practice schedule, performing it at least twice a week for one month, then once weekly on Saturday.

3. Integrate the Hebrew Letters and the Energy Body exercise into your practice schedule, performing it at least twice a week for one month.

4. Obtain one or more of the following resources and make a study of the meaning of the various letters. Draw them in your notebook, being careful to reproduce them as accurately as possible. See:

   - The Philosophers of Nature, *Qabala,* Lessons 37–40, by Jean Dubuis
   - *The Inner Meaning of the Hebrew Letters,* by Robert M. Haralick
   - *The Cipher of Genesis* and *The Second Coming of Reb YHSHWH,* by Carlo Suares

Chapter 4

Pathworking: Getting There from Here

Pathworking is the most commonly known aspect of modern Kabbalah, and also one of its least understood. Guided visualizations have long been a staple of meditation and hypnosis seminars, the most obvious advantage being that the group leader guides one or more people through a series of preselected symbols and ideas to a specific conclusion. Done as stories, not unlike fairy tales, they can be easily understood in light of Eriksonian hypnosis, in which stories are used to allow a certain amount of free association but also so that the story framework keeps the action moving to a conclusion. Thus, each person is allowed a certain degree of insight and personal revelation as they fill in details, while a broader construct of teaching is conveyed through the use of the general outline of the story.

> "Each fairy tale is a magic mirror which reflects some aspects of our inner world, and one of the steps required by our evolution from immaturity to maturity. For those who immerse themselves in what the fairy tale has to communicate, it becomes a deep, quiet pool which at first seems to reflect only our own image; but behind it we soon discover the inner turmoils of our soul—its depth, and ways to gain peace within ourselves and with the world, which is the reward of our struggles."
>
> **Bruno Bettelheim,**
> *The Uses of Enchantment*

Hasidic masters used storytelling as their principal means of teaching. The same idea is found in medieval morality plays and in ancient and modern temple initiations, such as one sees in high-degree Freemasonry—the difference being that in these settings, living human beings personify the roles and bring them to life, rather than the active and directed imagination of the listener.

Two of the most well-known examples of guided visualization for the purpose of assisting consciousness are the Tibetan Book of the Dead and the Egyptian Book of the Dead. The Tibetan Book of the Dead is read or recited to dying or recently deceased people to guide them in their journey through the intermediary realms to the pure light of awakened consciousness. The Egyptian Book of the Dead was recited as well, but moreover, its texts were written on the coffins and sarcophagi and inside the tombs of the deceased so that they would have directions on where to go and what to do. The Egyptians viewed hieroglyphs in the same manner as Kabbalists view Hebrew letters: as living beings. So, for them, this was the equivalent of having a person reciting the text for the deceased.

Any well-told tale is a Pathworking, either consciously or unconsciously. Classic movies and television shows offer us an insight into the needs of the human psyche for this kind of experience. In some ways, Pathworking is ideal for today's media-oriented culture, as it demonstrates the strengths and weaknesses of such a technique as well as its subtleness and the dangers for abuse.

The relationship between esoteric Pathworking and childhood fairy tales is well established. However, in our quest for individuation, self-reliance, and separation from our parents, social rules, and religious restrictions and sexual taboos, we abandon our childhood means of development for a more active one in the material world of experience. To guide us in picking our experiences, we leave behind our old fairy tales and choose new ones, such as the modern mythologies of television shows and soap operas, movies, and long-running musical shows. While most modern entertainment offers little genuine value and is designed mostly for the absorption of our life force and time, all forms of storytelling offer a moral lesson and cosmological view whether we recognize it or not. The same is seen, or heard, in the endless tales of suffering, failure, alcoholism, and neediness in country and western music and in the unrequited love in jazz and blues, with the protagonists turning toward drugs and alcohol as a result. Rap and heavy metal offer their own metaphors, cosmologies, and worldviews as well.

All that we watch, listen to, and participate in has the potential to be a Pathworking on some level. However, what separates such randomness and potentially harmful psychic exchanges from undesirable and chaotic suggestions is that Kabbalistic Pathworking is organized, progressive, and ultimately transpersonally oriented.

Initiation

The function of these esoteric or psycho-spiritual exercises is to make us aware in a broader sense of what we are—and what we may become if we so desire it. They are to assist us in fulfilling the Greek adage "Know Thyself in order to know the universe and the gods!" In our Becoming, the alchemist claims, *we realize that we are self-created beings.* We are directly or indirectly responsible for who we are and

> "Initiation essentially aims to go beyond the possibilities of the individual human state, to make possible the transition to higher states and finally to lead the individual beyond any limitations whatsoever."
>
> **Rene Guenon,**
> *Aspercus sur l'initiation*
> **(Glimpses of Initiation)**

what we experience in life, despite cries to the contrary. Each person, as the alchemical adepts say, is a "son of his works."

Until this century, the most common method of esoteric learning was either through a teacher-student relationship or through affiliation with an esoteric lodge. The principle means of instruction and initiation was often ritualistic and would involve one or more persons who had experienced the ritual or its equivalent previously. The initiator and/or initiatic team would proceed to create a condition in which the energies of the psyche would be awakened and brought to the surface of consciousness. For this to work effectively requires that those energies being awakened in the initiate already be alive and well in the psychic body-consciousness of the initiator. This is a critical point, and the failure of this condition being met is the principal cause for esoteric initiations as a whole being of questionable value. The best results occur when those teaching and initiating are also able to *do*.

These sudden flashes of insight and alteration of consciousness can in some instances be called initiations, some being minor and others more significant. Unfortunately, the concept of initiation in esoteric circles is filled with many misconceptions, and in psychology it has no equivalent term or phrase, although several might be suggested.[1]

Psychological Effects of Pathworking

The effects of Pathworking are to a greater or lesser degree well documented, with the commentaries by Israel Regardie (*A Garden of Pomegranates*) and Gareth Knight (*A Practical Guide to Kabbalistic Symbolism*) being the most easily available and reliable. Once you understand the basic concepts of what each sphere represents in terms of psychological elements on the Tree of Life, then you can realize the links that they form either through ritual, mythological metaphor, meditation, or a combination of the above. However, in the rush to realize magical powers, altered states of awareness, celestial beings, and interior worlds, seekers often overlook one of the most significant and important facts of Pathworking, and all magical work in general:

> "This you know. I am parched and perishing."
>
> *The Hymns of Orpheus*

The majority of all so-called magical, mystical, alchemical, or esoteric work, as much as 90 percent of it, is nothing more than glorified psychotherapy.

In fact, few people stay with any system long enough to realize the genuinely spiritual aspects of the work they are doing. Students must recognize the need for genuine self-honesty and purification on the level of the ego and the repressed areas of the subconscious if they are to derive full benefit from the work they are doing. Only then can the refined and powerful forces of the soul shine freely and effectively through the ego and not be overly distorted by it.

To this end, we give the following examples of Kabbalistic Pathworking, as well as possible psychological benefits or pathologies that their working

---

1 The writings of Karlfried Graf von Durckheim combine depth psychology, Christian mysticism, and Zen practices in such a fashion as to allow for the realization of one's interior life with Christ, a purpose in harmony with both psychosynthesis and traditional Western esoteric Pathworking. His writings are a significant contribution to this area—even though they use the language of orthodox Christianity—and are a valuable tool for bridging this gap between psychology and mysticism, and even esotericism.

(particularly out of sequence) can evoke within the psyche of the operator. While no single path is ever worked exclusively, but only realized as such by our outer self (i.e., the ego), we see the effects predominantly when particular paths are undertaken as ritual or esoteric operations. The paths are numbered in a working sequence for a reason; it is best to follow that sequence if disharmony and psychic disruption are to be held to a minimum. Each of us carries within us the seeds for healthy and unhealthy uses of the forces we are made from and contain. Whenever we approach a particular sphere or spheres, we also approach their reflection in the klippoth. The *klippoth* is nothing more than an imbalanced force or an excess of a particular virtue, to such a degree that it becomes a vice.

To be clear on this point, the paths are numbered, and their order should be strictly followed by the practicing Kabbalist until all of the paths have been completed at least once. This is done to maintain psychic harmony and to rebalance the energies as they are encountered and experienced. Once this is done, it will be considerably easier for the operator to take those very experiences and to direct them—either as a Pathworking or as another form of practice—in healing work for themselves or for another person (regardless of whether the recipient has done any esoteric work). Once the inner experience of the path is had, it becomes an integrated part of us and is always available for our use, just as one learns a new language and simply converses with another person without having to review grammar or vocabulary. Because the experience is "energetic" in nature, we are able to impart some of it to another person, in this instance, as part of a healing session.

If you seek to use a path for physical healing without proceeding through all of the paths of the Tree, or at least those leading to Tiphareth, you may do so only insofar as you make the firm and unwavering commitment that the purpose of your inner journey is to bring health, healing, and harmony into your body. This singular focus directs the energies and grounds the experience, thereby minimizing the potential negative side effects of performing the path out of order. While this is not the preferred method for an individual to be undertaking Pathworking as a solitary practitioner, it is acceptable in this context. In general, if you are not familiar with Pathworking and do not want to undertake it as part of your spiritual development but still wish to use it for healing work, it is preferred that you be assisted by someone who has some experience in this area to perform the path with you and guide you through it so that each step is clearly performed. An alternative would be to record the path and play it back to yourself so that you are fully engaged in the visualizations and not distracted by trying to remember each step of the process.

The Paths

The paths on the Tree of Life that follow the descent of Mezla return power and can be seen as more active and energetic in orientation; those paths that do not follow Mezla are sometimes seen as more passive and reflective in design. In reality, each combination of psychological potentialities, or Pathworkings, returns something to the consciousness of the mind traveling them. "Return" is not even the proper word, for such qualities have always existed in the soul, but only in *potential*. It is through the experiences of life incarnate and the desire—the need—to make sense of it through psycho-spiritual philosophies, techniques, and initiations that it becomes a reality, or *actualized in our consciousness*.

Those who have done esoteric work, particularly Kabbalah, will find that in the beginning the spheres and paths are very rigid entities. However, as one works with and internalizes them, they become more fluid and interrelated on a level that cannot be expressed in words. It is these progressive interior experiences that allow one to experience levels of spiritual initiation.

We say that these initiations are part of *progressive interior experiences.*

This is to distinguish the psychological, the mystical, the genuine transpersonal aspect of growth from the purely sensational. The experiences undertaken by students of Kabbalah, alchemy, or other Hermetic disciplines are *progressive*; that is, they build on the previous experiences and have a direction or purpose. They are *interior* states in that they are wholly personal, even if experienced in a group or in the presence of others. They may match the descriptions given by others in traditional writings, but they are the "property" of the one who experiences them. They are an internal response to the pleadings of the self for expansion and integration. They cannot be experienced for another, nor given to another, except by highly integrated individuals known as adepts. Even then, the gift is just the psychic equivalent of the "jump start" one gives to a dead or weak automobile battery on a cold day. They are also, as the word says, *experiences*—not thoughts, ideas, conjectures, or philosophical postulations, but experiences, often of a profound and energetically charged nature.

The paths are thirty-two in number, ten belonging to the spheres and twenty-two to the connections between them. They are arranged in hierarchical order, ranging from the most dense (thirty-second) to the least dense (eleventh). In the order given here, the names of the Sephiroth have been substituted with their planetary equivalents for those who are unaware of traditional Kabbalistic terminology.

All of the paths associated with Tiphareth or our solar element bring with them, on some level, the risk of spiritual pride. This is because the solar fire, the energy of our core being, as it reflects the Light of our Highest Self (God, if you will), empowers all that it touches. Thus, if not sufficiently cleaned out, our intellectual delusions and feelings toward self and the world will be exaggerated in Hod. Our passions and creative instincts and impulses, whether they be artistic, sexual, or simply emotional, will be exaggerated in Netzach. In Yesod, our sense of spiritual communion, purpose, and mission will be empowered or distorted depending on our degree of psychological health.

What can make this even more confusing is the lack of adequate language to describe the various states and levels of experience. We talk of one Tree, but Four Worlds, and envision a Tree within each world, or even each sphere. Fortunately, computer programs give us some useful metaphors to help explain the ancient metaphors we are using. Each sphere can be seen as a text inside of a greater file. Every time we open one, we have the opportunity in some fashion to open another related to it. Each sphere is like a "window" that, when opened, can cause an internal cascade of connections to other related "windows" or files. Only when we have fully explored all of the files (spheres) in a folder (world) are we able to see how it all hooks together. We create these internal files, folders, and windows so that we can digest the material in small pieces. In reality, we are working on all spheres and paths simultaneously; however, we only become aware of them one at a time. When we have attained a sufficient degree of understanding of all the spheres on a given level, then we are said to have working knowledge of that world. With each world, this knowledge, via experience, deepens, as does our degree of initiation. We are also given glimpses of what lies ahead at certain points along the journey. When we experience the harmony of the physical world, we get an impulse to sense what lies beyond it (the psychic, Yetzirah). When we experience the central unity of the emotional-astral world (Yetzirah), we get a glimpse of the awesome guiding intelligence behind it in the World of Briah. When the harmony of this world is experienced, we get a sense of what remains on our journey home. Thus, we can travel each path four times for all of the levels of possible experience. It is in the World of Yetzirah, however, that the most important part of our work is done. It is on the lowest path, those leading up to Tiphareth on some level, that we need to focus our attention if we are to go beyond the Veil of the Second Death and be of genuine service—and not just self-serving under the guise of spirituality.

All of the paths may be experienced on the level of Yetzirah, but not all of them are directly or principally concerned with it. Those paths leading to Tiphareth are concerned with the structure and purification of the ego, our sense of self, and how we deal with the world. Those paths leading from Tiphareth in the World of Briah are concerned with our expressing of those values in daily life as service and sacrifice. They are more concerned with the experiencing and directing of the energy of the soul (superconsciousness). The paths leading beyond the Abyss, and in the World of Atziluth, are concerned principally with contacting directly the undifferentiated energy of God (collective consciousness). This is why work on the lower paths is so critical. Those who jump to the higher paths or work them out of order risk triggering impulses within themselves and their environment that they will be unprepared for. The energy will not flow smoothly; it will eradicate blocks as it goes, and psychic, physical, or social ills may result from it. Once the energy hits a block, it will flow like water through whatever channel is available, be it a weakness or a strength.

Skipping the Center

Because of these blocks, some seek to avoid those conflicts and sacrifices that occur along the Path of Return. This is most dangerous when the initiate seeks to cheat Nature's demands and climb up the sides of the Tree, that is, enter the higher realms of self-awareness (Tiphareth) without having made the required sacrifice of the ego's dominant features. This happens when the path between Hod and Geburah or Netzach and Chesed is chosen prematurely.

The preference for which pillar to climb will most likely result in earlier preferences; that is, an opening of Netzach without Chesed will lead to a high-strung and irrational approach to one's endless material and sensual desires, but if Hod is open, then the probability of them manifesting is likely. Here one uses one's intellectual powers simply as a means to satisfy earthly desires and a lust for power.

If Hod is opened but Netzach isn't, and the energy flows out of the ego's fear of emotional power and need to be reduced in priority for the solar light to be more pronounced, then neuroses, anxieties, and fear will dominate, as the initiate only has the power of "well-laid plans" that never manifest. Since there is no real passion, even in the most selfish sense, there is no psychic or creative power present.

The problems then presented are simple. The power of the higher sphere must be abandoned and the proper corrections made, or the more highly refined psychic energies unleashed will fall like a weight on the unrefined and weak psychic structure below, reducing it to rubble. If the energy (under the direction of a panicking ego) seeks an escape from this "fall," then it can only increase the complexity of the issues stated by climbing to the top of their respective pillars; follow the course of *involution* not *evolution* on their return to Tiphareth; or attempt further premature path crossings, this time across the Abyss, resulting in possible long-term psychological damage.

The problem posed by the Abyss, or Daath, is that it represents Knowledge, or a state of awareness, that is not accessible to the limitations of the ego. That is, it is an access to unrestricted Deity and, as such, shatters all restrictions. On the descent, the energy coming through Daath begins to form the nucleus of our ego, so on the ascent, this same energy can only undo, or de-form, the ego if any is present. Daath is crossed several times, and it can even to some degree be seen in our experiences of our unconscious with its psychic, sexual, and repressed drives and inhibitions (Yesod). Here we are taken aback by the new world of dreams, fantasy, and psychic reality that awaits us, but we must first face the Terror of the Threshold. This terror, loss of control, and devastating encounter with genuine reality would only crush the ego we have so carefully built up over the ages—and our whole sense of being with it—if we did not first, slowly, layer by layer, undo and rebuild ourselves from self to Self. This is not to say that those who have crossed the Abyss *in some form* do not have egos or a sense of self in the world, but that through training, experience, and maybe even divine grace, they have been able to temporarily set it aside so that they may enter into higher states of awareness.

Summary

To undertake the task of the Path of Return, we need to recognize the many facets of our psyche, how they relate to one another and interact, and the problems and potentials that are set forth at each step of the journey. To this end, the Tree of Life is a useful diagram, map, and tool. Only in its application, however, do we find the subtleties that exist within us. By "making haste slowly," we can unravel the tangled web of our interior life so that the Inner Light, the Light of Initiation, can be revealed.

Using the Paths

The twenty-two connecting paths have an additional set of "invisible" paths that are not included in any of the traditional literature but which can be worked out by experienced students on their own. Simply look at two spheres that could have a path between them but do not; there you have the location of an "invisible path."

For our purposes, only the paths below Beauty (Tiphareth) will be examined. These relate to the problems of the ego and the body, as well as the related psychological disturbances that often link and affect both of them. This trinity of "self," body, and unconscious forces of rational thought, emotions, and instincts is the main area of work in all spiritual systems.

The paths themselves have less of a healing property, as that is really the domain of the elements and the planets, but instead unite diverse energies and create conditions and contexts in which healing is more likely to occur. However, as we will see, certain paths need to be functioning well for any healing to take place.

Traditionally, using the paths for healing purposes has been very straightforward. Each path has an elemental, planetary, or zodiacal correspondence, and it is this relationship that has been used to establish the healing properties of the paths. This is a simple, direct, and effective method of working with the paths, and any experienced Kabbalist will instantly recognize the reasons for the relationships given. However, this process ignores the influences of the spheres that form the terminals of the path. Both systems will be presented here, with the difference being not in their execution but in the results the operator and/or recipient desires from the experience. Less depends on what you do than on what you intend to do. Your intention, or Will, is everything. The following list of the paths and their influences over the parts of the body is a good place to start and is taken from the correspondences used within the Hermetic Order of the Golden Dawn. For additional diseases covered by the paths, consult a work on traditional Western herbalism in which the astrological and planetary rulerships of the organs are listed. The finest work on this to date is *Culpeper's Medicine: A Practice of Western Holistic Medicine*, by Graeme Tobyn. Anyone seriously interested in working with traditional Western holistic healing, wherein the importance of zodiacal and planetary forces is utilized, must read this book.

Traditional Correspondences of the Paths for Healing Work

Path	Influence	Body Part(s)
11th	Air	Respiratory organs
12th	Mercury	Cerebral and nervous system
13th	Moon	Lymphatic system
14th	Venus	Genitals (female)
15th	Aries	Head and face

(continued on page 111)

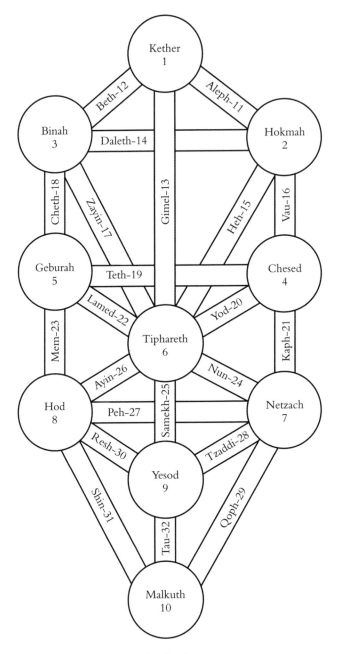

The Paths

Traditional Correspondences of the Paths for Healing Work (*continued*)

Path	Influence	Body Part(s)
16th	Taurus	Shoulders and arms
17th	Gemini	Lungs
18th	Cancer	Stomach/Womb
19th	Leo	Heart
20th	Virgo	Back
21st	Jupiter	Digestive system
22nd	Libra	Liver
23rd	Water	Organs and nutrition
24th	Scorpio	Intestines
25th	Sagittarius	Hips and thighs
26th	Capricorn	Genitals (male)
27th	Mars	Muscular system
28th	Aquarius	Kidneys and bladder
29th	Pisces	Legs and feet
30th	Sun	Circulatory system
31st	Fire	Organs of circulation (increased energy to the heart)
32nd	Saturn/Earth	Excretory system

If you would like to work with a particular path but are unsure if it is appropriate, check the general description of the planetary or astrological influence given above and compare it to the illness you seek to address. You may end up doing more than one path. At some point, however, the choice may not always be clear-cut and you will have to trust your intuition on which path, given its energy, will be more appropriate for the condition being addressed. The additional information given below may also assist in identifying which paths to use for releasing emotional and mental blocks as well.

NOTE: When doing Pathworking for spiritual purposes, we address the relationship of the spheres of each path from the lower sphere to the higher one. When addressing the paths for physical health, we address the spheres from the higher one to the lower one. From the health perspective, our desire is to draw energy down along the Path of Mezla (Creation) and not simply traverse the Path of Return in search of some possible and undetermined psychic experience. *It is very important that the intention of returning with energy for a change in consciousness and physical health be firmly implanted in the subconscious of the operator and all participants when preparing for this kind of Pathworking; this intention must be reinforced once the Sphere of Completion is reached and before the return journey has begun.*

Thirty-second Path

This path governs our connection to the invisible, but also dreams, phobias, and irrational concerns or obsessions. It helps us to overcome our fear of death to some degree, as well as understand how our inner worlds affect us and direct so much of our decision-making through the filters of mental and emotional imbalances. This path is also concerned with fundamental survival issues and governs sexual reproduction, birth and death, conception, solidification of things, the etheric body, anything requiring connection to the physical world, and issues of the bowels and urinary tract, such as constipation. This path is a good general tonic for the psychic-etheric-physical body connections.

Thirty-first Path

This path governs our rational thought process and mental clarity, as well as metabolism. It also is concerned with all aspects of regeneration, purification, and increased energy flow into the psychic and physical bodies.

Thirtieth Path

This path is concerned with the exchange of information between our conscious, rational, concrete mind and our subconscious. When functioning properly, it allows for increased spiritual insights and has a profound effect on the psychic centers (the heart and pituitary in particular), increasing the rate of exchange of psychic information—although mostly in dream states and via symbolism. This path is exceptionally good for the heart, solar plexus, and thyroid, and for releasing unresolved issues around the sense of self.

Twenty-ninth Path

This path governs the influence of the emotions and endocrine system on the body. It is good for the kidneys as well, in their role as an organ of purification.

Twenty-eighth Path

This path is concerned with the effects of the emotions on the subconscious and thereby on the physical body through repressed emotions and conflicting emotional states. This is good for fertility and sexual performance issues.

Twenty-seventh Path

This path directs the emotional and rational energies together, thereby creating a mechanism for material life. It harmonizes them via the solar plexus and is therefore good for anxiety and extreme nervousness, as well as physical issues in the stomach, abdomen, and bowels. Its also has a profound effect on the general energies of the body for physical well-being, and therefore is good for addressing issues of fatigue, blood disorders, and circulation.

Twenty-sixth Path

This path is concerned with the relationship between our concrete mind (daily rational and cognitive thought) and higher thought, specifically the direct spiritual experiences of intuition and clairvoyance. It affects the nervous system—with emphasis on the brain, but also the thyroid through its relationship to Mercury—and is good for those doing dream and sleep practices.

Twenty-fifth Path

This path is concerned with the relationship between our personality and our true sense of self. It brings the nervous system into balance and awakens the general healing ability of the physical and psychic bodies as a whole.

Twenty-fourth Path

This path is concerned with the relationship between our emotions and higher influences. Through this path, our human expressions can be expanded—or our divine aspects can be reduced to ego-satisfying behaviors. Through its influences on Venus, this is a path of purification. It affects the kidneys, skin, and sexual organs, but also the heart on several levels simultaneously, and secondarily it affects excretion (as a result of purification). This path brings harmony to whatever is brought to it, with a strong influence on physical life and health.

Twenty-third Path

This path affects the entire circulatory system, including the lymph, and is concerned with purification. It is a water path that utilizes the energies of Mars and Mercury combined, making for swift and powerful actions on the world of form. The water aspect directs those energies toward our emotions, as well as any aspect of our physical health involving circulation.

Twenty-second Path

This path is concerned with the balancing out and harmonizing of our physical energies with our emotions and our sense of self. Because of the intense emotion and conflict that this path can symbolize, it is very good for those who feel the need to always be pleasant and nonthreatening, only to explode or run from conflict at a later point. Issues of the heart, symbolically and literally, are what this path addresses. Through it, physical health (Mars) can be brought to strengthen the will and the sense of self as well as the physical heart (Sun) through finding true inner balance, or imperturbability (Libra).

Twenty-first Path

This path affects our ability to expand and assimilate our capacity for health and well-being as a whole. In this aspect, it is one of the most important paths on the Tree as far as physical health is concerned. Jupiter is health and general wellness acting on itself, thereby multiplying its influence into our daily life through Venus—emotional and physical harmony. Therefore, the powers of Venus are multiplied and expanded. Once again, the powers of the body to harmoniously purify itself should be enhanced (as opposed to the more rigorous effects of the twenty-third path), and overall coordination improved. Assimilation in terms of digestion and respiration will also be affected. This path is concerned with the long-term effects of our daily actions on our health.

Twentieth Path

This path is concerned with the relationship of Jupiter, the powers of expansion, and the self through the human intellect or mind. As such, it is also concerned with the relationship between the heart (Sun) and lungs (Jupiter) and the rapidity of their interchange (Mercury).

Nineteenth Path

This path is concerned with the relationship of the organs of assimilation with the circulatory systems and the heart. As a rule, it is a powerful path ideal for providing strength before any operation, as a part of recovery, and for daily work. This is a very important path.

Eighteenth Path

This path is concerned with the movement of powerful psychic currents (Saturn) into the circulatory and muscular systems (Mars). Additional effects are on the bone marrow, lactation, and the ovaries (Cancer). For problems of conception or gestation, use this path, and also use it for any healing requiring a steady flow of powerful, materializing energy over a sustained period of time.

Seventeenth Path

This path is concerned with the movement of powerful psychic energies (Saturn) into the heart (Sun) and the awakening to higher levels of consciousness. This path will give a kind of resurrection experience in times of sudden crises or near-death experience in physical terms. Because of the influence of Gemini, the thyroid can be affected, as can the upper part of the lungs. This path will induce an irrevocable change in one's life course.

Sixteenth Path

This path is concerned with the influences of our personal horoscope (the Wheel) on our material life (Taurus) and our ability to expand and grow (Jupiter) from it. It is best done when there is an unknown cause of illness or when various treatments are unable to take hold.

Fifteenth Path

This path is concerned with the influence of our horoscope on our personal life path and our ability to create it. This path is good for those who are not ill but may be lingering in a state of confusion or even outright depression and despair. The influence of Aries gives both a strong directional quality to the results and the energy to accomplish goals.

Fourteenth Path

This is a powerful path and is concerned with how our horoscope impacts the ability to take form. This can be useful for troubling pregnancies and births and for understanding premature births.

Thirteenth Path

This is a powerful path that expresses our relationship of healthy individuality to the Divine. It affects the various psychic centers and endocrine glands in the brain, particularly the pineal and pituitary. This is very good for assisting those who are dying, in that the energies are concerned primarily with the heart (Sun) and brain (Kether) for the dissolution of the elements.

Twelfth Path

This path is concerned with the ability of the body to absorb psychic energy and transform it harmoniously into its four primary etheric streams, or elements: fire, air, water, and earth. This path is for those who are unconscious or in a coma and hanging on with no hope in sight. It should be done with paths 19, 18, and 21. This path can also help if a person is lingering in a protracted death process by working the path according to Return to assist in dissolving the elements.

I No.	II Hebrew Letter	III English	IV Pronunciation (Letter Name)	V Meaning	VI Joining Sephiroth	VII No. Value	VIII Path on Tree	IX Astrological Symbol	X Tarot Trump
1	א	A	Aleph	Ox	Kether to Hokmah	1	11	♒	0. The Fool
2	ב	B, V	Beth	House	Kether to Binah	2	12	☿	I. Magician
3	ג	G, J	Gimel	Camel	Kether to Tiphareth	3	13	☽	II. High Priestess
4	ד	D, Th	Daleth	Door	Hokmah to Binah	4	14	♀	III. Empress
5	ה	H	Heh	Window	Hokmah to Tiphareth	5	15	♈	IV. Emperor
6	ו	V, O, U	Vau	Nail	Hokmah to Chesed	6	16	♉	V. Heirophant
7	ז	Z	Zayin	Sword	Binah to Tiphareth	7	17	♊	VI. The Lovers
8	ח	Ch	Cheth	Fence	Binah to Geburah	8	18	♋	VII. Chariot
9	ט	T	Teth	Serpent	Chesed to Geburah	9	19	♌	VIII. Strength
10	י	Y, I	Yod	Hand	Chesed to Tiphareth	10	20	♍	IX. Hermit
11	כ	K, Ch	Kaph	Spoon★	Chesed to Netzach	20	21	♃	X. Wheel of Fortune
12	ל	L	Lamed	Whip	Geburah to Tiphareth	30	22	♎	XI. Justice
13	מ	M	Mem	Water	Geburah to Hod	40	23	▽	XII. Hanged Man
14	נ	N	Nun	Fish	Tiphareth to Netzach	50	24	♏	XIII. Death
15	ס	S	Samekh	Prop	Tiphareth to Yesod	60	25	♐	XIV. Temperance
16	ע	O – nasal	Ayin	Eye	Tiphareth to Hod	70	26	♑	XV. The Devil
17	פ	P, F	Peh	Mouth	Netzach to Hod	80	27	♂	XVI. The Tower
18	צ	Tz	Tzaddi	Fish Hook	Netzach to Yesod	90	28	♒	XVII. The Star
19	ק	Q	Qoph	Back of Head	Netzach to Malkuth	100	29	♓	XVIII. The Moon
20	ר	R	Resh	Head	Hod to Yesod	200	30	☉	XIX. Sun
21	ש	Sh, S	Shin	Tooth	Hod to Malkuth	300	31	△	XX. Judgement
22	ת	T, S★★	Tau	Tau Cross	Malkuth to Yesod	400	32	♄	XXI. World

★ More often it means "palm of the hand."

★★ In the Ashkenazic dialect, Tau can be pronounced as "s." In the more common Sephardic dialect, Tau is pronounced as "t" or "th."

Eleventh Path

This path is to assist those who are either coming into or going out of this world. It should be done in connection with the thirty-second path. The path is traveled according to Mezla for birth and according to Return for death.

The Practice of Pathworking

The actual practice of Pathworking can be as simple or as complex as the operator desires. Traditionally, when a path or mystical technique was being described to students, it would not be uncommon for teachers (rabbis) to actually be inwardly performing the practice and describing their experiences to the students seated around them. This creates a sort of initiatic environment where the experiences and increased energy of the teacher were extended outward and those listening could be affected by them. To some degree, the same occurs in a well-performed ritual initiation; however, since many of our readers will be working alone or in small groups, it is important that the process be kept simple and easy to perform often.

Keep in mind that repetition is the key to changing our inner perspective of things. The more we practice these basic methods, the easier it will be to understand the pattern being presented and thereby find our way in the higher realms of the Tree of Life. The following is the generic pattern for Pathworking. Write it down and study it so that you understand what is going on and in what order. The remainder of this chapter will give detailed examples of this technique in practice, along with its possible applications for healing. These examples will be limited to those paths leading from Kingdom (Malkuth) to Beauty (Tiphareth). If these examples are practiced and thoroughly assimilated, then students will easily be able to replicate the process for the remaining paths.

Exercise—Pathworking

Explanation—Pathworking establishes a conscious working relationship between the different spheres of the Tree of Life. This is done within our aura and, as a result, also within our subconscious, etheric, and even physical levels of being. If done properly, Pathworking can be a valuable tool for psychological wholeness and even physical wellness.

Type of Practice—If Pathworking is going to be used as a healing technique, then it must become a core practice for the practitioner, in that each of the paths must be traversed at least once prior to their being used as a healing modality.

Preparation—The practitioner and recipient should prepare themselves with several minutes of relaxation, prayer, and purification practice as previously given. Establishing the psychic centers or establishing the Tree of Life with a quick run-through of the Middle Pillar or Flashing Sword is desirable, but this can be omitted if there is insufficient time.

Method—After preparations are complete, proceed as follows:

1. Imagine your sphere filled with light.

2. Form the Sphere of Origin. This is the sphere or Sephirah in which the Pathworking begins or from which it originates. In the example beginning on page 121 it is Malkuth; in other Pathworkings, it may be other spheres.

3. Invoke the power of the Word. The power of the Word or primitive power of material creation is invoked through a statement of intention and the addition of speaking the divine names of the sphere.

4. Imagine a doorway before you. On it is the symbol for the path you are to tread, and you walk over to it, place your hand on the door, and open it. Only you can open the pathways to the inner world; no one else can do it for you, nor do they open from the inside without your consent.

5. See a vast plane of colored light stretching into the infinite. In the distance is the planet or symbol of your destination.

6. Before you is the tarot card of the path, fully alive, animated, and three-dimensional. You examine it closely and note its details.

7. You walk along the path, noticing a Hebrew letter for the path you are on, as well as its planetary, zodiacal, or elemental sign. This tells you the gift of this particular path.

8. Walk toward the main symbol of the card and address the characters or pay attention to any message they may have for you.

9. Move past them or it, and pass through toward the Sphere of Completion.

10. The planet or symbol is small but grows larger as you approach.

11. As you get closer, everything disappears until it fills your inner screen.

12. Walk into it and be absorbed in its light.

13. Reverse the journey.

14. Close the door.

15. Affirm the success of your journey, invoking the power of the Word.

16. Open your eyes and wake up.

The basic process for Pathworking does not change. It can be made more complex and sophisticated by adding opening, intermediary, and closing rituals. The most basic Pathworking and the most complex will both have the same three fundamental elements: (1) a Sphere of Origin, or starting point; (2) a Sphere of Completion, or goal; and (3) the path linking the two, whereby a synthesis is created, transcending both the spheres and the path as individual entities. However, regardless of the degree of sophistication, what matters most is the attitude of the operator. Openness, confidence, and a genuine desire to experience the inner realms to bring healing, strength, and wholeness into your life, or to those being assisted, are essential.

It is important to remember that the paths below Beauty (Tiphareth) on the Tree of Life represent the ego and its relationship to creation. The paths above Beauty represent how the ego relates to spiritual realities. The paths leading specifically to the Holy Upper Trinity (The Crown, Wisdom, and Understanding, or Kether, Hokmah, and Binah) represent extremely abstract spiritual energies and the domains of pure undifferentiated consciousness.

Incorporation into Daily Practice—Each of the paths, at least up to and including all those that link to Tiphareth, should be done by the practitioner prior to working with them as a healing modality with others. Even after a path has been ritually experienced, its key symbols and experiences must be meditated upon and integrated over the following week. Ideally, each path should be the primary focus of the student's practice for one month.

Examples of Pathworking

The Thirty-second Path

The thirty-second path is the primary means by which energy enters into the physical world and, for ourselves, our physical body, which makes this path critical to understand if we are to develop any healing skills. It can be used as a general tonic for healing when it is not clear what other path or paths to use, and it can be used in conjunction with them if they are known.

The Pathworking

1. Imagine a sphere of light surrounding you and the recipient.

2. Imagine the symbols of your Sphere of Origin around you. For Kingdom (Malkuth), a black-and-white checkerboard-paved floor is sufficient. Other symbols can be added later if desired. Imagine the symbol of the sphere in the floor beneath you, as if it were in tile and you were standing on it.

3. State your intention or purpose for undertaking the journey:

   "I, _____, undertake the journey of the thirty-second path of the Tree of Life, from the sphere of Kingdom to the sphere of Foundation, in the names of Adoni ha-Aretz and Schaddi El Chai, united by the power of YHVH Elohim, for the purpose of _____. This is my will. So Mote It Be! Amen!"

4. Imagine a doorway before you. On its lintel is a keystone engraved with the Hebrew letter Tau, the symbol for the thirty-second path. You walk over to it, place your hand on the door, and open the door.

Only you can open the pathways to the inner world; no one else can do it for you, nor do they open from the inside without your consent.

5. See a vast plane of indigo light stretching into the infinite. In the distance is a large full moon in its brilliant glory, reflecting the light of the inner sun.

6. Before you is a maiden, nude but for being wrapped in a winding cloth of red and green. She twirls two wands, and each wand is capped by a blue and red sphere. On closer examination, you see that they alternate between colored light and then fire and water—the active and passive principles in creation constantly at work.

7. The maiden stands in the center of what appears to be a large wreath, which is shaped like an eye turned on its side. This is the entrance to the womb of eternity.

8. You walk along the path and notice a Hebrew letter Tau and the planetary sign for Saturn. This path promises to unite the inner and outer worlds within you and to teach the secrets of making the innermost wishes and desires concrete.

9. Walk toward the maiden. Ask her an important question, but only one question with each session. You can also ask her help in bridging the seeming gap between the inner and outer worlds, for she is your Inner Self, pure and undisguised. She wields the powers of creation.

10. Move through the wreath and her, enter into her and pass through, toward the moon.

11. The moon is small but grows larger—even the phases of the moon appear around it, like crescents pointing out from around the rim.

12. As you get closer, the crescents disappear and only the moon remains. See it as brilliant silvery white, with a hint of violet. Walk toward it until it fills your screen.

13. Walk into it and be absorbed in its light. Imagine that you are standing on a floor made of a silvery white, or moonstone color, and are inside a large, nine-pointed star with a crescent moon in the center, at your feet. Be receptive to any images or sounds you may experience. When you feel it is time to return, affirm that you are taking with

you the powers of the sphere for the intention stated at the beginning of the ritual.

14. Reverse the journey.

15. Close the door.

16. Affirm that your journey was successful:

"I, _____, have tread the thirty-second path of the Tree of Life from Malkuth to Yesod, in the divine names of _____ and _____, united by the power of _____, for the purpose of _____, and returned. My will is done. So Mote It Be! Amen!"

17. Open your eyes. Ring a bell, clap your hands, or stomp your foot to become clearly grounded and awake. Make a short notation in your journal regarding the ritual and its results. Note the date, time, and lunar phase under which the ritual took place.

Comments on the Formula

1. This formula can be made more powerful by the addition of various divine names and names of angelic forces. However, simplicity is best, and complexity only adds power if the reason for its use is understood. Experienced students will easily understand the application of the Rituals of the Pentagram and Hexagram as part of Pathworking, and new students should consider learning these rituals for addition to the path after they have become familiar with the basics outlined here.

2. The tarot cards suggested come from the Universal Marseille Tarot deck, taken from one of the oldest known decks in existence and the basis for most modern decks. However, the images are crude, and beginners may feel more comfortable with the Rider-Waite deck. The Tarot of Bologna is almost identical to the Marseille deck and is a suitable substitute. The Wirth deck is richly colored and very appropriate, but the assignment of Hebrew letters to the cards follows a different order than is typically seen, and so this deck should not be used for the purposes of this particular work. Complex decks, such as the Thoth-Crowley deck, and non-Kabbalistic decks should not be used, as simplicity is a keynote to this particular expression of Pathworking.

3. Assumption of the Godforms for the Spheres of Origin and Completion can be used; however, it is sufficient to assume the imagery of the principal figure on the path, as it is the path's guardian. Merging with the imagery awakens its corresponding energies in our psyches and thereby allows the power of the path to flow. If one is seeking a generic Godform to use for all Hermetic, Kabbalistic, and healing work, one can do no better than to use Thoth, the Egyptian god of magic and alchemy. If a non-Egyptian form is preferred, a brilliant angelic figure, such as depicted on the tarot card for Balance, is also appropriate.

4. When you reverse the journey, pause when you come across the principal figure of the tarot card, and even become the figure once again, to see if there is any additional message to be conveyed. It is important that the return not be rushed, so proceed at a smooth and comfortable pace so that you may remember and assimilate the energies and experiences.

5. When you are in the Sphere of Completion, you may imagine a small chest at your feet or before you. Open it and see what is inside. If nothing comes into your imagination, simply visualize yourself taking out a small wrapped package, bag, book, or Elixir-filled vial. Take it back with you and allow your dreams or later meditations to reveal what "gift" or "power" you received from the journey. Relax and don't be concerned about it; just know that the ritual has positive effects every time it is done.

6. The closing affirmation of success is important for beginners, as it acts as a reinforcement of the purpose of the ritual. Experienced students may decide to retain it or discard it, but those new to Pathworking, especially Pathworking aimed at creating change in the material world through healing, should retain it until experience dictates otherwise.

7. The ringing of a bell, or some other form of noise to firmly shift consciousness back to the material world, is critical.

8. It is important that, as a student, you take notations of these practices so that they can be fully integrated into your memory and psyche. Information may be given over a period of days, weeks, or even months, and only with accurate notes can you fully piece together and utilize it.

How to Use Pathworking in a Healing Session

Pathworking is easily incorporated in a healing session in which either the healer performs the Pathworking as part of the healing process and the recipient simply is receptive to its influences, or the healer and recipient perform the Pathworking together and the recipient actively visualizes and takes part in the process.

Preparation

1. Perform the Practice of the Six Directions to stabilize the elements and affirm your relationship to them and origin in the Void, expression through the Ground of Becoming, and harmonization in the Central Place of the Spirit. If you are pressed for time, it is acceptable to start with a simple prayer or blessing.

2. Stand behind the recipient with both hands on the shoulders of the recipient, thumbs and forefingers close to the spine if possible. It is acceptable for both recipient and healer to sit on a chair or stool so that both are in optimum states of relaxation.

3. Have the recipient relax by leading a brief relaxation and breathing program lasting two to three minutes. Then proceed with the Pathworking.

The Pathworking

1. Imagine a sphere of light surrounding you and the recipient.

2. Imagine the symbols of your Sphere of Origin around you. For Kingdom (Malkuth), a black-and-white checkerboard-paved floor is sufficient. Other symbols can be added later if desired. Imagine the symbol of the sphere in the floor beneath you, as if it were in tile and you were standing on it.

3. State your intention or purpose for undertaking the journey:

   "I, _____, undertake the journey of the thirty-second path
   of the Tree of Life, from the sphere of Kingdom to the sphere
   of Foundation, in the names of Adoni ha-Aretz and Schaddi El
   Chai, united by the power of YHVH Elohim, for the purpose of
   _____. This is my will. So Mote It Be! Amen!"

4. Imagine a doorway before you. On its lintel is a keystone engraved with the Hebrew letter Tau, the symbol for the thirty-second path. You walk over to it, place your hand on the door, and open the door. Only you can open the pathways to the inner world; no one else can do it for you, nor do they open from the inside without your consent.

5. See a vast plane of indigo light stretching into the infinite. In the distance is a large full moon in its brilliant glory, reflecting the light of the inner sun.

6. Before you is a maiden, nude but for being wrapped in a winding cloth of red and green. She twirls two wands, and each wand is capped by a blue and red sphere. On closer examination, you see that they alternate between colored light and then fire and water—the active and passive principles in creation constantly at work.

7. The maiden stands in the center of what appears to be a large wreath, which is shaped like an eye turned on its side. This is the entrance to the womb of eternity.

8. You walk along the path and notice a Hebrew letter Tau and the planetary sign for Saturn. This path promises to unite the inner and outer worlds within you and to teach the secrets of making the innermost wishes and desires concrete.

9. Walk toward the maiden. Ask her an important question, but only one question with each session. You can also ask her help in bridging the seeming gap between the inner and outer worlds, for she is your Inner Self, pure and undisguised. She wields the powers of creation.

10. Move through the wreath and her, enter into her and pass through, toward the moon.

11. The moon is small but grows larger—even the phases of the moon appear around it, like crescents pointing out from around the rim.

12. As you get closer, the crescents disappear and only the moon remains. See it as brilliant silvery white, with a hint of violet. Walk toward it until it fills your screen.

13. Walk into it and be absorbed in its light. Imagine that you are standing on a floor made of a silvery white, or moonstone color, and are

inside a large, nine-pointed star with a crescent moon in the center, at your feet. Be receptive to any images or sounds you may experience. When you feel it is time to return, affirm that you are taking with you the powers of the sphere for the intention stated at the beginning of the ritual.

14. Reverse the journey.

15. Close the door.

16. Affirm that your journey was successful:

   "I, _____, have tread the thirty-second path of the Tree of Life from Malkuth to Yesod, in the divine names of _____ and _____, united by the power of _____, for the purpose of _____, and returned. My will is done. So Mote It Be! Amen!"

17. Open your eyes. Ring a bell, clap your hands, or stomp your foot to become clearly grounded and awake. Make a short notation in your journal regarding the ritual and its results. Note the date, time, and lunar phase under which the ritual took place.

To use this Pathworking formula with other paths on the Tree of Life, it is important that you be familiar with the basic function of each of the spheres. If you have not spent any time in meditation on the spheres and their rudimentary meanings, or performed the exercises previously suggested in chapter 3, particularly the Flashing Sword, integrating Pathworking will be difficult. The following rubric will help outline the information needed to utilize this model as a template for additional paths. It is important to have a complete list of Kabbalistic correspondences, such as those outlined in *Self-Initiation into the Golden Dawn Tradition*, by Chic and Sandra Tabatha Cicero, and *The Golden Dawn*, by Israel Regardie. Dion Fortune's *The Mystical Qabalah* is also helpful in this area. The Roman numeral notations in the following paragraphs show where the information can be found in Aleister Crowley's *Liber 777*.

Pathworking Template

1. Imagine a sphere of light surrounding you and the recipient. This establishes an area of work and concentrates the energy being used in the process.

2. Imagine the symbols of your Sphere of Origin around you. This can be as simple as visualizing the geometric symbol of each sphere, or imagining a primary symbol as if it were in tile beneath your feet. This image connects and grounds you to the beginning and end of the visualization and should be firmly visualized. (Column XLIX, XLVIII, or XLI)

3. State your intention or purpose for undertaking the journey:

   "I, _____, undertake the journey of the [insert the number of the path] path of the Tree of Life, from the sphere of [insert the name of the Sphere of Origin] to the sphere of [insert the name of the Sphere of Completion], in the names of [insert the divine name of the Sphere of Origin] and [insert the divine name of the Sphere of Completion], united by the power of [insert the divine name of the path], for the purpose of _____. This is my will. So Mote It Be! Amen!" (Column V)

   If you do not know the divine name of the path, simply state the Hebrew letter of the path.

4. Imagine a doorway before you. On its lintel is a keystone engraved with the Hebrew letter assigned to the path you are working. You walk over to it, place your hand on the door, and open the door. It is important that you imagine yourself opening the door, as it is an act of will, of personal choice, that you are undertaking this journey.

5. See a vast plane of light in the primary color of the path stretching into the infinite. In the distance is a symbol of the Sphere of Completion. You can see your way, where you are going, and all that lies in front of you. (Column XVI)

6. Before you is the tarot card of the path, alive and in three dimensions. This card contains the principal challenges and benefits of the journey. Through it, the powers of the Sphere of Origin and the

Sphere of Completion are synthesized and made available to you for the work being undertaken. (Column XIV)

7. You walk along the path and notice the Hebrew letter of the path stretched out before you, and you imagine that you are actually walking on the letter, that it carries you to your destination. The planetary and elemental signs of the path are also visualized and trod upon (Column VII). Contemplate the reason for your journey, what it is you desire to attain as you move forward.

8. Walk toward the main character as pictured on the tarot card and in your mind's eye. Ask he or she an important question, but only one with each session. It is important to be still and receptive after asking the question. However, move on regardless of whether you are aware of an answer or not, as it will most likely come later in the session or while dreaming.

9. Move past the figure and through the remaining images of the scene and on toward the Sphere of Completion. Visualize it getting larger as you approach. Walk toward it until it fills your entire screen of vision.

10. Walk into the Sphere of Completion and be absorbed in its light. Imagine that you are standing on a floor dominated by the sphere's symbol. Be receptive to what images or sounds you may experience. When you feel it is time to return, affirm that you are taking with you the powers of the sphere for the intention stated at the beginning of the ritual.

11. Reverse the journey.

12. Close the door.

13. Affirm that your journey was successful:

> "I, _____, have tread the [insert the number of the path] path of the Tree of Life from [insert the name of the Sphere of Origin] to [insert the name of the Sphere of Completion], in the divine names of [insert the divine name of the Sphere of Origin] and [insert the divine name of the Sphere of Completion], united by the power of [insert the divine name of the path], for the purpose of _____, and returned. My will is done. So Mote It Be! Amen!"

14. Open your eyes. Ring a bell, clap your hands, or stomp your foot to become clearly grounded and awake. Make a short notation in your journal regarding the ritual and its results. Note the date, time, and lunar phase under which the ritual took place.

Ficino and Renaissance Psychotherapy

Marsilio Ficino was a fifteenth-century priest and physician whose work *Libri de Vita* was first published in 1489 and subsequently became the most popular of all his writings. Like most medical texts of the Middle Ages and the Renaissance, Ficino's work liberally used astrological symbolism and methods for prescribing cures for various diseases. Just as genetics would be taken for granted in a modern medical text, in Ficino's period, astrology would be as well.

What set Ficino apart, however, was his suggested use of talismans for the curing of diseases (in particular *melancholy*, a disease ruled by Saturn), which bordered on crossing the fine line into magic in an era when even the accusation of such practices could cost one his reputation or life.

Ficino's natural magic was similar to many of the ideas put forth by psychologists today, only he structured it in the language of the period *and* had genuinely magical (i.e., Neoplatonic/Greco-Egyptian) applications through the use of talismans.

In summary, Ficino stated that we are, or become, the images that we surround ourselves with, and that we can "draw down the life of the heavens" through the application of plants, food, scents, colors, and animals that correspond to a particular planet (i.e., quality) we seek.

Ficino prescribed for his clients that they surround themselves with the images of universal harmony, as well as those representing particular virtues. Paintings, murals, mechanical clocks of the solar system—anything the mind could imagine was to be put to the use of reminding the observer of the underlying influences it represented. In fact, Ficino and his contemporaries would go so far as to say not just *represented*, but *incarnated*, thus moving Ficino from pure psychology into magic.

Crossing this threshold from pure practical psychology into the realms of magic is a critical step, both internally and externally. In doing so, Ficino, or one practicing his "prescription for what ails us," no longer is just a passive participant in creation, but rather an active agent in its unfold-ment. The powers move from being a closed, internal, personal experi-ence to becoming an interchange with cosmological forces accessible to all of us.

The same theory of association and connecting *spiritus* was applied to music and song through singing the invocations of the Orphic Hymns.

Most of the images suggested by Ficino are similar to those presented in the *Picatrix* and are composed mainly of planetary symbols with the ancient gods in their normal forms. The use of these mundane images is justified, as his practices work only with the "worldly forces" and not "demonic" or "spiritual" ones, and are thus "natural magic."

Thomas Moore points out in the introduction to his work *The Planets Within* that for Marsilio Ficino, the soul pervaded and embraced every-thing. To encounter the soul and its power, Ficino suggested the use of images, like so many Hermeticists before and after him, and suggested the constant and regular use of imagery. Psychological health for Ficino could even be measured in the degree that a person used imagery in his or her life and had a well-nourished imagination—not unlike our latter-day psychotherapist and magician Dr. Israel Regardie, who is often quoted as saying, "Invoke often!"

The principal idea behind Ficino's psycho-spiritual Hermeticism is in the practice of experiencing an imminent deity. By recognizing our psychological tendencies through astrology (or reflection or therapy), we can begin to develop our strengths and minimize our weaknesses. This is done primarily through experiencing those qualities we seek to embody through association.

If we surround ourselves with beauty, we become beauty. If we sur-round ourselves with wisdom, we become wisdom, and so forth. Images are formed in the mind, and as much as possible, created in the material world. Thus, Divinity is not limited to abstraction and flights of fancy, but made incarnate in our daily experiences.

In the ritual setting, the decorations of the temple will often be colored, scented, and resounded, with those things most closely associated with the spheres and planets involved in the Pathworking. Images both internal and external will be imagined and created to focus the consciousness on the task at hand. Here we see a direct connection between Renaissance magic, modern magical Pathworkings, psychology, and initiation.

Key Points

- Pathworking is an inner journey using symbols to tell a story and stimulate deeper levels of awakening.
- Modern Pathworking is often unrelated to traditional forms, in that modern schools overlay so many varieties of symbols, mythologies, and systems that one suffers from a sort of symbolic bulimia.
- Pathworking has specific physical healing qualities but is generally not used for that purpose.
- Pathworking is traditionally done in a specific order and looks for specific inner experiences.
- Pathworking can be used to address specific mental and emotional issues as well as physical ones.
- Pathworking can allow an individual to experience high degrees of interior integration and wholeness, leading to increased creativity, psychic health, and physical well-being.
- Over time, because of the progressive interior experiences that Pathworking can provide, it can also increase lucid dream states and projection of consciousness and assist in the experience of genuine interior initiations.

Assignments for Chapter 4

1. Obtain a copy of one of the following tarot decks: Rider-Waite, Oswald Wirth, or Marseille. Since you will want to imbue it with your personal vibrations, keep this deck only for meditation and Pathworking and allow no one else to touch it. Study the major trumps at the rate of one card a week, starting with the Fool, followed by the Magician, and continuing in numeric order to finish

with the Universe (also known as the World). Simply sit in front of the card for a few minutes each day and allow your eyes to pass over it. Close your eyes and visualize the card for a minute or two, and then put it away. This is a very passive method of absorbing the images of the cards, and there is to be no effort or strain, only relaxation, as if you were gazing at a distant mountaintop or valley. If you choose to "remember" your vision of the card as you are falling asleep, the images will be further implanted into your subconscious and will positively affect your dream state. You may choose to come back to any card or cards after you have completed working with each of them individually for one week.

2. Some students who are unfamiliar with Pathworking and Kabbalah in general may find the minimalist approach presented here difficult to follow without a broader framework to place it in. If this is the case, obtain a copy of Israel Regardie's *A Garden of Pomegranates*. Read about the first three paths and study their formula of construction. Perform the paths in your imagination as instructed, and later dissect them down to their key components. Once completed, return to the formula rubric presented here and compare your list of key points to it.

Meditation Practices for Chapter 4

1. Perform a meditation or full ritual as described in this chapter on the thirty-second path once a week, on Mondays, for a month. Note your experiences. The thirty-second path is the main path, or mechanism, for becoming aware of the flow of energy between the physical and subtle worlds. A thorough understanding of this path is extremely important. Proper awakening of the thirty-second path will give rise to increases in lucid dreaming, astral projection, and the mechanics of the etheric body. Monday is the day ruled by the Moon, and it maximizes the effects of any work or meditation on this path.

2. Meditate on what mastery of the material world would mean to you. What are its benefits? What are its responsibilities? We are in the physical world to become fully aware of our True Self through the work of overcoming the inertia of physical life. By mastering the details of the finite world of matter, we master the inner world of the infinite. This is one of the understandings of alchemy.

3. Proceed to work each of the paths between Malkuth and Tiphareth (thirty-second through twenty-fifth) at the rate of one path per month until all are completed. Note your experiences. The paths given are the most important group of paths we can encounter in our desire for integration and the ability to heal ourselves and others of physical and emotional maladies. The majority of our illnesses have to do with our perceptions of ourselves and how we relate to others and the physical world. These paths are directly concerned with helping us bring clarity and harmony to our personality and daily life so that the powerful rays of the Inner Self bring a healing warmth rather than the burning fires of purification if contacted prematurely. A solid understanding born of experience on these paths will make any work on the remaining paths self-evident.

Chapter 5

Kabbalistic and Alchemical Physiology

Kabbalah is a system of cosmology based on symbols and their relationship to everything from abstract ideas about the beginning of the universe to human psychology, events in the physical world, and the psychic essence that binds it all together. At times, the number and types of symbols used, not to mention their combinations, can be overwhelming. It seems almost as if Kabbalists try to be so obscure, difficult, and outright confusing that they want people to throw up their hands in despair and walk away. But this is not the case. The confusion, in fact, comes as a result of several different Kabbalistic systems developing over at least one thousand years, and as a result of attempts by modern Kabbalists, both Jewish and non-Jewish, to find meaning in esoteric doctrines that appear very much out of their original context.

The original context is based in the concept that the world—indeed, the whole cosmos—is interpreted as being interrelated and connected. To affect one part is to affect the whole in some manner. It was developed at a time when thoughts, words, and images were considered as alive and potent as are the physical forces that modern physics calls gravity, magnetism, attraction, repulsion, and so forth.

With the onset of the Renaissance, modern science began to develop, but a holistic view was still maintained. Only with the advent of the late seventeenth century do we see the beginning of the separation of the various areas of learning into specific and increasingly isolated disciplines. This separation gave rise to specific and distinct advantages that cannot be ignored, as it has since led to the high standard of living that most readers of this book appreciate. However, the natural and necessary outgrowth of it was an increased focus on material causes and effects, to the detriment of the spiritual. It is easy to understand why this happened when we consider the violent and irrational oppression that early experimenters, inventors, and other seekers of wisdom encountered. Doctrines and ideas were not to be countered with demonstrable facts, and anyone who did so was in jeopardy. The list of early martyrs in the cause of science is well known and is the source of much of today's equally irrational antagonism between science and religion.

As such, it is important that we, as practical Kabbalists, seek to put ourselves in the proper frame of mind. Thus, we can begin to experience creation as a continuum of vibration and consciousness from the most subtle to the most dense, the whole of which is connected through the consciousness of each of us. Through symbols, sounds, and emotions, we can create a ripple that moves out and touches similar and sympathetic vibrations, which in turn create a cascading set of causes and effects across the fabric of the visible and invisible universe.

In short, each of us is a universe in miniature and interacts with other miniature universes as well as the larger universe as a whole. In Kabbalah, this great connection is symbolized by the Tree of Life, with each Being reflecting a part or all of the powers, intelligences, and expressions of the Tree.

To understand how this perspective affects magical operations in Kabbalah, it is important to understand the relationship of the human aura to the body, to the psyche, and to the universe. Only with this understanding can we begin to realize how much of our world is literally lived within our own "skins" as well as our own "little world." By recognizing the filtering effect of the aura, we can begin to attune it—and thus ourselves—to the various powers and potencies that open us up to other worlds, other beings, and our True Self.

Spend as much time as you need on this section. Read it several times, pausing to visualize the ideas presented. In imagining these ideas, you will make them a part of yourself and begin the process of experiencing the great simplicity, despite appearances of complexity, that Kabbalah offers.

The Beginning: The Sphere of Sensation

Everything projects from the Void, or Nothingness, into Kether. From Kether, it then descends through a series of reflections, creating the various planes of consciousness and matter that we call the spiritual and material worlds. While these two worlds appear at times to be very separate, they are in fact two halves of a whole and must always be addressed that way if they are to be understood.

These projections, or spheres, as they are called in Kabbalah, exist on innumerable levels. Practical Kabbalists, because of their need for simplification, focus their attention on the ten primary spheres and how they move energy between the invisible and visible worlds.

Beginning with the only thing each of us truly has—our own body and mind—Kabbalists examine every phenomenon of mind and body, of the visible and invisible, as reflected in their personal aura. They realize that the aura, or *Sphere of Sensation*, as it is called, is the means whereby our physical bodies are created and sustained. The aura is also the means of transmitting and receiving psychic impressions of the world around us, including those of the astral planes.

The importance of the aura or Sphere of Sensation for practicing Kabbalists cannot be understated. It is their means of bringing energy into the body, as well as the filter or mechanism that allows them to energetically interact with others, either for healing or for initiation. To describe it crudely, the aura is the shell of the light bulb, the consciousness is the voltage of the light bulb, the cosmic is the energy source or electricity, and the personality is the brilliance of the bulb or the actual light that gets through.

Using the same analogy, light streams out of the pores of the body. It is this energy that is registered when we experience an intermingling of auras such as during a healing session, ritual work, or initiation. In a healthy person, this energy fills the space between the physical body and the outer shell of the aura. In the average person, it does not extend very far. In a healthy person, it extends, but it may or may not reach the shell, focusing on the physical aspects of life. In the adept, this energy reaches the auric shell and creates a reflexive condition like a touch screen on a modern cash-machine monitor, enabling the adept to attune their consciousness to similar patterns and ideas. We must strengthen our aura, expand our aura, and understand our relationship to our aura if we are to make magic work.

Within the aura, the adept builds, through visualization, a series of symbols that are imprinted on it. These act as intermediaries for the various levels of energy, matter, and consciousness the adept is contacting. The primary symbol for us is the Tree of Life, which is built through exercises such as the Middle Pillar and the Lightning Flash. Here, the "Tree" takes on a three-dimensional quality. It creates a series of pillars that reach from above our heads (Kether) to below our feet (Malkuth). These connect the abstract energies of the invisible with the dense energies of the material and those various degrees in between. Because these symbols are imprinted on the aura as the energy passes through the physical body—and this is a critical point—the Sphere of Sensation is also referred to as the "Magical Mirror of the Universe," as it is our personal reflection of the universe in miniature.

In this manner, Kether forms the crown of our head, with Hokmah and Binah forming the left and right halves of the brain and head. Chesed and Geburah form the left and right shoulders and arms, Tiphareth forms the chest and torso, Netzach and Hod form the left and right hips and legs, Yesod forms the organs of reproduction and excretion, and Malkuth forms the feet, and notably also the whole of the physical organism.

From this perspective, the psychical body is seen as standing between four pillars, emanating light and moving within a giant sphere. The four pillars are the Tree of Life in three dimensions, or placed so that it can be seen "face on" from any view, save the top, which is always Kether, and the bottom, which is always Malkuth. The pillars are static, as are Kether and Malkuth, but the human body moves (and they with it like a chariot), and the outer shell or surface of the aura is constantly changing. The most powerful of forces acting on it is the zodiac, as the aura contains the static imprint of an individual's natal chart, which becomes activated as it is impacted by various astrological influences, some of which it will be in harmony with, and others with which it will not.

Each area of the body is given to an aspect of consciousness. Each aspect of consciousness interrelates with the others just as the organs of the body interrelate with each other. This is then projected through the body onto the Sphere of Sensation as a motion-picture projector projects a movie onto a screen—a screen that can only be seen with the psychic eyes and felt with the psychic body.

This form of expression is very personal. For that reason, the energies, which are by nature impersonal, are often given personal qualities, extracted from our subconscious. They are given human form when we interact with them as they course through our consciousness and physical body. If we understand ourselves and how these energies affect us, we can then understand others, as well as the whole of creation. For this reason, the aura of the student is the mirror into the student's own soul, and the soul of Being.

The energies in the aura are in constant flux as a result of our thoughts, feelings, actions, and astrological conditions, as well as the elemental tides. By creating a strong focal point in the center of all this activity, we are able to reach out and direct the energies as we would like, and we also gain the ability to be unperturbed by events and activities around or inside of us. This focal point is our personal seat of consciousness, found in the sphere of Beauty (Tiphareth), and from this seat of power are directed the various psychic and physical energies. This direction can manifest in the form of a conscious and enlightened ruler, or in contrast it can result in neglect and ignorance of the spiritual plane through a focus on materiality. The choice is ours, as we are the king who sits on the throne. It is our decisions that affect the energies of our heart and, from there, our entire being.

The pillars of the Tree of Life are astral symbols built up to concretely represent the very real etheric energies pulsing through our body, primarily through that portion of the nervous system that is near as well as within the spinal column. Because Kabbalah does not traditionally directly address the energies of the body in the same way that Eastern systems do, symbols are used to mediate between the body and mind. They are then supplied with emotional energy to make the connection complete. Symbols impact the mind, not the body, and they need emotions to do that. The greater part of occult training is learning how to energize symbols with emotions so that they will be effectual.

Eastern systems use symbols as well, but in a more concrete fashion, as can be seen in tantric practices in which sexual energies are directly engaged and sublimated. While this is becoming more common in Western practices, it has yet to be fully integrated to the same degree as in the Eastern systems. For this reason, anthropomorphic images are essential in that they arouse an emotion within us that brings energy to the activity. Without this energy, symbols are dead, and esoteric practices worthless.

The Nephesh

In Kabbalistic literature, the focal point of the Nephesh is confusing, as it cannot be limited to a single "location." It is in fact a conduit of energy between the dense world of matter and the subtle world of psychic energy. One source clearly places it in the sphere of Foundation (Yesod), whereas another places it in Kingdom (Malkuth). If we examine the function of the Nephesh, it is clear that it is *based* in Yesod but *extends into* the material world, giving life and movement to it. For this reason, we have said that the etheric is a subset of the Nephesh, whereas one Kabbalistic authority states that the etheric *is* the Nephesh.

This latter statement is perfectly acceptable given that the Nephesh, like the etheric, provides form and structure upon which to construct the physical body (Guph) and gives the physical body the energy of motion. One Old Testament saying is that "the life is in the blood." This is sometimes translated as "the soul (consciousness) or instinctual consciousness (Nephesh) is in the blood." This may be considered correct, for, as we have seen, the life force travels the path of least resistance and is found in abundant amounts in the blood, lymph, and sexual fluids. From the bloodstream, the life force feeds denser organs of the body. Thus, one may place the etheric body as being a sub-part of the Nephesh, or as being the Nephesh itself. In general, it can be seen as being focused in the dense psychic realms (Yesod) but most active in the material world and physical body (Malkuth).

The Etheric Body in Healing and Magic

In the teachings of the Golden Dawn taken from the Zohar, it is clear that the Nephesh has two functions: one, as we have described, is fixing the subtle energies into the physical body, and a second is similar to the astral body that can project and be separate from the physical body for a period of time. From this we can say that there is a "higher Nephesh," or an etheric body that relates to the sphere of Yesod, and a "lower Nephesh," or an etheric body that is strictly the framework the physical body is built on and nourished from.

The solar plexus seems to be the most commonly referred-to physical location where they meet and interact. The solar plexus acts as a general psychic and physical tuning fork for the body (taking the energy generated from centers below and distributing it), as well as the most common place for projection of consciousness, or astral projection.

From the solar plexus, the etheric energy and lower-pitched psychic energy is distributed across the etheric body into the physical, as well as its connecting link to the astral, through the seven primary psychic centers, or chakras, and their corresponding nerve plexuses in the body.

The primary function of the Nephesh, or etheric body, is to regulate and pass on energy, and also information, between the physical and psychic planes. This works in both directions, as energy that is directed toward the body produces health and well-being. The energy that is directed toward the higher pitch of the etheric, or lower psychic, produces visions, flashes of psychic response, and clairvoyant images, particularly in response to persons or objects in close proximity.

On an energetic and psychological level, the etheric body deals exclusively with creative energy. While this is referred to as libido, or sexual drive, the quality and quantity of energy utilized is far more than physical. Its creative power is not limited to forcing the union of egg and sperm. This creative impulse is what lies behind every action we undertake—and even our very drive to be. It is the hidden psychic seed forcing our Becoming through action.

When we act, we create, if only in some small way. When we do not act, we are dead, inert, or impotent. We can still our body to create with our mind, just as we can still our mind to drive energy into the body to create with it, either through sex or through activities in the physical world with physical tools and products. Whatever it is, this energy is in us. It continues to flow into and through us, and it must be utilized, or blockages are created. These blockages become the basis for physical and mental-emotional illness, as has been documented by Freud, Jung, Reich, and others.

This etheric energy is absorbed from two places: the nutrients we consume as food and the air we breathe. From our food, our body derives nutrition and takes in the etheric energy of the plant or animal eaten. This energy can only be used for physical health. As the saying goes, "You are what you eat." Etheric energy from the air comes from the energies of the sun, which vitalizes the air and, in turn, vitalizes us as we breathe. This is easily demonstrated by the fact that the energy of the air, or niter of alchemy, is highest in the spring and summer months. As such, the etheric energies of the air are affected by astrological cycles. This energy is unified as it emanates from the sun and is polarized upon reaching our atmosphere. This polarity gives rise to what we call the elements, or four divisions of etheric energy: fire, air, water, and earth.

It is easy to see, then, as this energy forms the four dense vibrations that give rise to physical life. Their energies are individually identifiable and yet are so intermingled that an experienced adept can "breathe in" the etheric elements of water and earth for emotional and psychical health just as easily as eating chocolate or a nutritionally rich meal. We can also see why alchemists keep referring to the Secret Fire hidden in the earth. This fire is both the real molten core beneath the earth's mantle and the solar energies that condensed to form all of life as we know it.

Because the etheric energy is further refined into the various elemental expressions, it is also affected by the flux and cycle they experience across the day and across the year. This daily fluxing of energy begins with sunrise, reaches its apex at true noon, or the actual midpoint of the sun across the sky, and continues into the evening and night. This divides the day into four major zones, each with its dominant element or etheric energy. Each of these zones can further be subdivided through groupings of hours and minutes, ad infinitum to the point at which the cycles happen so frequently that they are useless on the practical level. This is identical to the idea of planetary hours, except it uses the elemental (etheric) energies rather than the planetary pulses.

From this it can be easily understood why color, sound, and smell (the core elements of ritual) affect the etheric body, first through the emotions of the astral and then into the etheric and then physical body, as well as why physical stimuli of heat, warmth, cold, wet, or dry affect the body and, through it, stimulate the emotions in the reverse direction. By understanding these interactions and using them consciously, we become more efficient in our daily life and take greater control of our health and happiness.

One of the more interesting aspects of the psychic body as it relates to the physical form is the concentration of energies around the heart and the radiation of energies from the hands and fingers. These two points have the greatest of practical applications in spiritual healing for ourselves and others.

The Heart

The heart is the means whereby the etheric energies of the sun, absorbed through the air, enter into the bloodstream and circulate to the organs of the body. It contains the most powerful energies in the body next to the sexual organs. When combined, these two sources of material (earth and water) and spiritual (fire and air) energy create the Philosopher's Stone within the human body. In them, the body becomes the Philosopher's Stone.

The Hands

The hands are the chief means of projecting energy into the world, both physically and psychically. Just as each side of the body has a dominant charge of negative or positive, so does each hand. Each hand also has dominant fingers. Eliphas Levi stated that the thumb and first two fingers of each hand are the most powerful for emitting energy, and as such they are the most often used in blessings and healings, as can be seen on icons and religious statuary. Each finger also has a dominant charge of etheric energy.

Knowing this, we can be specific in the type of energy we are giving to a person, if need be, and we can also know where to find its source. Earth and water will come primarily from Malkuth, as will the passive aspects of breath; fire and air and the active aspects of breath will come from Kether. In short, a sort of Hermetic *pranayama* can be easily developed to demonstrate this relationship of the etheric elements to the breath and their root source.

Various Uses of the Hands in Healing

Exercise—Healing Hands: The Universal Position for Prayer

Explanation—This exercise brings the active and passive energies of the body together, opening the psychic centers of the hands and fingers, as well as those of the heart and upper body. It is ideal as a preparatory practice in itself prior to any form of contact healing involving therapeutic touch.

Type of Practice—Preliminary exercise for healing sessions.

Preparation—Prepare yourself in any manner you choose from among the previous exercises given.

Method—After you have prepared yourself, proceed as follows:

1. Hold your hands about six inches from your chest at the level of your heart, elbows down, shoulders relaxed (you may use the armrest of a chair if needed), and fingers tilted slightly upward. Your palms should be comfortably apart, as if a small ball were between them.

2. With your eyes closed, breathe in slowly and deeply, holding the breath for several seconds before exhaling.

3. As you exhale, imagine that a stream of bluish-white or silver-blue energy flows from your heart-chest area through your arms and into your fingers, enveloping your hands in a brilliant, firmly distinct aura of light.

4. Continue with this practice for five to ten minutes.

Incorporation into Daily Practice—This exercise should be done daily for at least two weeks to help generate an increased flow of energy into the arms, hands, and fingers. After several weeks, an automatic flow of energy will be established, which you will be able to feel whenever the hands are brought together. As such, simply holding this position for several minutes while doing other preparatory exercises, prayers, or meditations is a simple and effective way to incorporate it into daily practice.

Exercise—Sign of the Adept

Explanation—This exercise differs slightly from the previous one, in that while it brings the active and passive energies of the body together, opening the psychic centers of the hands, fingers, heart, and upper body, it does so primarily through energizing the heart. Like the previous exercise, it is ideal as a preparatory practice in itself prior to any form of contact healing involving therapeutic touch.

Type of Practice—Preliminary exercise for healing sessions.

Preparation—Prepare yourself in any manner you choose from among the previous exercises given.

Method—After you have prepared yourself, proceed as follows:

1. Place your left hand over your heart and your right hand over your left, with your elbows down and your shoulders relaxed.

2. With your eyes closed, breathe slowly and deeply, holding the breath for several seconds before exhaling. Visualize a brilliant reddish-gold flame in your heart. Feel its heat and radiance, like a sphere or a small sun.

3. As you exhale, imagine that a stream of red or red-gold energy flows from your heart-chest area through your arms and into your fingers and envelops your hands in a brilliant, firmly distinct aura of light before re-entering your heart.

4. Continue with this practice for five to ten minutes.

Incorporation into Daily Practice—This exercise should be done daily for at least two weeks to help generate an increased flow of energy into the arms, hands, and fingers. After several weeks, an automatic flow of energy will be established, which you will be able to feel whenever the hands are brought together. As such, simply holding this position for several minutes while doing other preparatory exercises, prayers, or meditations is a simple and effective way to incorporate it into daily practice.

In addition to using both hands in healing or to generate energy, you can use each hand by itself to direct a specialized current of energy for healing and initiatic purposes. Just as the right side of the body is considered active, male, and solar in its dominant qualities, so the left side is considered receptive, female, and lunar. You can generate and direct these active and passive currents to reinforce the active elemental energies of fire and air or the passive energies of water and earth, in relation to the elemental, planetary, or zodiacal correspondences you are using in treatment.

Exercise—Active Treatments Using the Right Hand

Explanation—This exercise strengthens and directs the active energies of the body for use in healing practices.

Type of Practice—Preliminary exercise for healing sessions.

Preparation—Prepare yourself in any manner you choose from among the previous exercises given.

Method—After you have prepared yourself, proceed as follows:

1. Hold your hands about six inches from your chest at the level of your heart, elbows down, shoulders relaxed (you may use the armrest of a chair if needed), and fingers tilted slightly upward. Your palms should be comfortably apart, as if a small ball were between them.

2. With your eyes closed, breathe slowly and deeply, holding the breath for several seconds before exhaling.

3. As you exhale, imagine that a stream of bluish-white or silver-blue energy flows from your heart-chest area through your arms and into your fingers, enveloping your hands in a brilliant, firmly distinct aura of light.

4. Feel as though your hands were the polar ends of magnets: your right hand expansive and dynamic, your left hand receptive and constricting. Feel as though a powerful ball of energy were being formed between your palms from these two polar energies.

5. After two or three minutes, place your left hand at your side. Using the right hand, imagine that this powerful, dynamic, electrical energy is moving through it toward the area being treated.

6. Continue with this practice for five to ten minutes.

7. After you have developed skill in the above method, begin to imagine that the active energy takes on the elemental quality of fire, and later air. Use only one element in each practice session until you achieve sufficient skill.

Incorporation into Daily Practice—This exercise should be done daily for one week to help generate an increased flow of active energy to the right arm, hand, and fingers.

Exercise—Active Treatments Using the Left Hand

Explanation—This exercise strengthens and directs the active energies of the body for use in healing practices.

Type of Practice—Preliminary exercise for healing sessions.

Preparation—Prepare yourself in any manner you choose from among the previous exercises given.

Method—After you have prepared yourself, proceed as follows:

1. Hold your hands about six inches from your chest at the level of your heart, elbows down, shoulders relaxed (you may use the armrest of a

chair if needed), and fingers tilted slightly upward. Your palms should be comfortably apart, as if a small ball were between them.

2. With your eyes closed, breathe slowly and deeply, holding the breath for several seconds before exhaling.

3. As you exhale, imagine that a stream of bluish-white or silver-blue energy flows from your heart-chest area through your arms and into your fingers, enveloping your hands in a brilliant, firmly distinct aura of light.

4. Feel as though your hands were the polar ends of magnets: your right hand expansive and dynamic, your left hand receptive and constricting. Feel as though a powerful ball of energy were being formed between your palms from these two polar energies.

5. After two or three minutes, place your right hand at your side. Using the left hand, imagine that this powerful, constricting, form-giving, magnetic energy is moving through it toward the area being treated.

6. Continue with this practice for five to ten minutes.

7. After you have developed skill in the above method, begin to imagine that the active energy takes on the elemental quality of water, and later earth. Use only one element in each practice session until you achieve sufficient skill.

Incorporation into Daily Practice—This exercise should be done daily for one week to help generate an increased flow of active energy into the left arm, hand, and fingers.

The hands can be used alternately, with the left hand pulling out energy blocks and the right hand dissolving them. The left hand can also be used to work with denser energies, such as earth, to help in the speedy recovery of breaks and bruises, and the right hand can be used to bring energy, vitality, and strength into the system.

Key Points

- Kabbalah requires that we view the universe as existing as one continuous stream of ideas, energy, and forms in an unbroken chain.
- This "Chain of Being" is accessed indirectly through symbols and their relation to specific parts of the human body, the psyche, the

physical world, and the invisible realms currently beyond day-to-day human perception.

- The human aura, or Sphere of Sensation, is the means whereby we experience consciousness. All ideas, experiences, emotions, and sensations are filtered through it, creating our understanding of experiences and our personal perspective.

- The lower Nephesh, or instinctual and unconscious self, is the key to all occult operations, as it provides the energy and connection to the material world needed for our imagined desires to manifest.

- The etheric body is a conduit of energy and form wherein material experiences are built. It controls the flow of the elemental energies and links the unconscious and material worlds (Yesod and Malkuth) as well as the unconscious and ego, or sense of self (Yesod and Tiphareth).

- The body has areas that correspond to specific elemental energies that can be used in healing by specifically directing those energies to afflicted areas of one's own body or another's body.

- The hands are the primary means for transferring energy to objects, animals, or other people.

Assignments for Chapter 5

1. Our physical bodies are made up primarily of water, and water covers most of the earth's surface. Next to fire, no other "element," or form of material expression, is as important as water. Over the last twenty years, a great deal of research has been done on the effects of thoughts and emotions on water and its ability to hold a physical and psychic charge even when extremely diluted. For this reason, spend some time researching the physical and healing qualities of water.

2. Confidence is critical when attempting to heal ourselves or someone else. Confidence can only be gained through experience. For this reason, practice each of the exercises in this chapter daily as described. Record your results in your notebook. Pay special attention to how your own body reacts to the exercises, as this experience will

be similar to how others will be experiencing your healing treatments with them. The better we understand how the energy acts on us, the better we can understand how it will act on others.

Chapter 6

Color-Coding Your Health

Esoteric physiology is complicated by a variety of different systems, each representing a different approach to the questions of what the human constitution is and how it relates to the cosmos.

It has become common in New Age circles to speak of the "four bodies"—the physical, emotional, mental, and spiritual bodies—as if they exist as separate vehicles rather than as a seamless extension from the most subtle to the most dense of our existence. This continuous unity must be kept in mind when dealing with energetic healing.

If we examine their fundamental makeup, we see that in Kabbalistic psychophysiology the physical body (Guph) is an extension and expression of the emotional (instinctual) body (Nephesh). The emotional body relates to the mental body (Ruach), the domain of reason and conscious decisions, which in turn relates to the spiritual body (Neshamah), or immortal, pure consciousness. The spiritual body is given several subfunctions or specific means of expression that are unique to it and that influence the other intermediary bodies of consciousness. These functions are Intuition

(Neshamah), Highest Will (Chiah), and Divine Spark (Yechidah). The Divine Spark is our pure seed consciousness, free of any intermediary bodies, vehicles, or expressions. It is Divinity in Being that expresses itself through the Highest Will, or our fundamental evolutionary impulse, which communicates its desires to an open and receptive consciousness through Intuition. However, for our purposes, our main concern is with the first four bodies or expressions of consciousness.

Body	Level of the Soul	Element	Action	Function
Physical	Guph	Earth	Gravitation	Solidity
Emotional	Nephesh	Water	Constriction	Fluidity
Mental	Ruach	Air	Expansion/Organization	Connectivity
Spiritual	Neshamah	Fire	Energy	Consciousness

So then, where is the etheric? It is a subset of the emotional and physical that overlaps both bodies.

How do the seven principle psychic centers relate to the above? Simply as energy modifiers. Each relates to a planet, an energy frequency or modulation, and as such, while having a preference for a specific element (such as Mars for fire or Mercury for air), they impact *all* of the levels.

The four bodies represent the four Adams, one in each of the Four Kabbalistic Worlds, with the last one being the one that "fell" and took on physical form. The four elements correspond to each of the Four Worlds and have their reflections in each other. Each world is a reflection of that which comes before and after it, with a particular emphasis on a single mode of expressing consciousness and energy (element) that tinctures all experiences in that world. Each of the seven planets relates to a phase of creation (i.e., Days of Creation) as well as a tuning or modulation of the principal elements. This is best understood in astrological terms, in which each sign has a planetary ruler and an element assigned to it.

Etheric Energy

The Four Kerubim, or Holy Living Creatures, are also the four rivers of the Garden of Eden, and they represent the coalescing and solidification of spiritual energy into material form.

They act as the subtle framework for matter to be attracted to (if such already exists in Malkuth/Assiah) as well as the framework upon which it is formed (if it is coming into existence out of Yesod/Yetzirah).

They bind and hold energy together (as such, they are closely related to the gravitational force of elemental earth) but are fluidic and belong to a subtle energy that connects them to the invisible. It is best to think of the visible and invisible worlds as two overlapping spheres at this junction where etheric is neither one nor the other, but both.

You affect the etheric and you affect the physical; you affect the physical and you affect the etheric.

The ethers tend to concentrate in organs of the body, as seen in the Egyptian Canopic jars, but there is little agreement on the attributions of various schools.

Earth Ether tends to hold the entire organism together via the skeletal structure and through the functions of the heart.

Water Ether tends to concentrate in the sexual fluids (but also in the endocrine system) and the spleen as a means of purification.

Air Ether tends to concentrate in the nervous system as well as organs of respiration or absorption.

Fire Ether tends to concentrate in the blood, liver, and brain.

All of these "ethers" are radiated from the sun in our solar system, reflecting as it were the most basic primordial energies of Unity (Kether) and the seed ideas of the four elements or ethers as seen in the Four Holy Living Creatures. They are identical to the four pranas of yoga. The sun is the source of these energies, distributing them in balance and harmony via the planets. This combination of planetary and pure elemental energy creates the relationships we experience as the zodiacal signs.

These are just generalizations, and it is important that each student experience the nature of the complex relationships of these energies that create and hold our body together.

"As above, so below. All from the One Thing."

Creation: "In the Beginning . . ."

Traditional Egyptian creation myths are numerous, but they all can be summed up in the idea that out of "nothingness" a god or goddess self-creates itself. This god or goddess then either creates other gods and goddesses who perform the act of creating the known universe, or the self-created one forms it as well. This often is seen as a mound of earth surrounded by, or coming out of, the primordial waters. Fire arises and has its own island of fire, with air separating earth and heavenly water. A similar story is found in Genesis.

"That which comes from the heart of the macrocosm comforts the heart of man—gold, emerald, coral; that which comes from the liver of the macrocosm comforts the liver of man."

Paracelsus

"The physician heals by their presence. Physician, first heal thyself!"

Paracelsus

During the Renaissance, Jewish mysticism, or Kabbalah, became the central focus around which much Hermetic cosmology was built and understood, and alchemy became its central practice. Astrology crossed over, as it was concerned with personal as well as cosmological questions and shared symbolism and applications with both systems.

The following exercise will help you identify the relation of the various organs, tissues, and functions of the body to the psychic heart. Using the healing, creative, and dynamic power of your "inner sun," you will purify the energy of these organs utilizing color, emotion, and sound.

"The Sun rules the heart.
The Moon rules the brain.
Venus rules the veins.
Saturn rules the spleen.
Mercury rules the liver.
Jupiter rules the lungs.
Mars rules the gall."

—*Correspondences according to Paracelsus*

While the above is good for starters, there are additional correspondences that are important for the variety of conditions that one may encounter:

Sun

All life is sustained by the powerful magnetic radiations of the Sun. The Sun rules the mind, the sense of self, willpower, energy, integration, wholeness, anything having to do with organization, and personal power.

In the physical body, the Sun rules the heart, circulation, the spinal column, general wellness, distribution of heat, the thymus gland, *pons Varolii* (control of breath), and the eyes (right in men, left in women).

In conjunction with Saturn, Virgo, and Scorpio, the Sun rules the spleen; the (sexual-etheric) energies transformed by the spleen are carried to the solar plexus for distribution to the entire body.

The Sun is masculine, libidinal, and conscious.

Organic, structural, or constitutional diseases arise from a lack of solar energy.

Moon

The Moon collects the solar energy across the year as it moves through the twelve signs of the zodiac. The Moon rules growth, fertility, conception, birth, family life (especially motherhood), the subconscious and psychic life (dreams), natural rhythms and instinctual life, and also reflection, passivity, and meditation.

The Moon rules the breasts (and lactation), the stomach, the womb and ovaries, menstruation, the bladder, urination, and all fluids, including those of the endocrine system and their transformation. It also rules the esophagus and thyroid (with Mercury and Scorpio), the pancreas, the brain as a whole, the cerebellum, memory, and the tonsils (with Taurus).

The Moon is changeable, familiar, feminine, and motherly, with a mix of bright and dark traits of kindness and raw instinct.

Cyclic diseases, irregular menses, and any of the lunar organs are under the Moon's influence.

Mercury

Mercury is associated with Hermes, the patron of medicine. Mercury rules the intellect, mediation (bringing together of opposites via Gemini), transmission of information, translation, mental and nerve processes, speech, writing, manual skill (dexterity), aloofness, and distribution of energies.

Mercury rules the nervous system (with Uranus), organs of hearing and speech, nerves in the arms (movement) and abdomen (assimilation), organs of respiration, mind-body coordination, the feet (as movement), the brain (with the Moon), the thyroid, nerve endings in any area, and the sensory organs. The Sun-like cerebrum and the Moon-like cerebellum are linked via the Mercurial pons.

Venus

Venus is related to alchemy and spagyric practices. Art, harmony, proportion, integration of separate parts into a whole (seven into one) and opposites (via Libra), music, and luxury are ruled by Venus.

Venus rules the metamorphoses of cells and the transformation within cells and tissue (fermentation and fertilization), particularly the skin and face; it also rules the reproduction and enhancement of substances (such as perfumes or spagyric tinctures), and as such the sense of smell. Venus rules the preservation of the physical body, the kidneys, the parathyroid, the thymus, the stomach veins, the internal sexual organs, the female breasts (when not lactating), the appetite, the intestines, the process of elimination, the palate, and to some degree the spine.

Mars

Mars is powerful, with its effects being either constructive or destructive. It accelerates and intensifies whatever comes into contact with its active and dynamic energy.

Mars rules the muscular system, body heat (with the Sun), the red corpuscles of the blood (blood strength and purity), the male sexual organs, adrenaline, sexual drive, the suprarenal glands, and the formation of blood (with the Sun and Jupiter).

Combined, the Sun and Mars bring vitality, courage, and initiative. The vital processes are ruled by Mars, in connection with Jupiter, Leo, Libra, Scorpio, Sagittarius, and Virgo. The motor nerves, the gall, the left brain, the left ear, the head, and head injuries are also influenced by Mars, as are the Secret Fire and the astral body. The process of elimination, inflammation, and surgeries are under its domain. Instinctual energies for procreation and self-preservation are ruled by Mars; as such, it influences so-called animal magnetism, or the etheric body and energy.

Jupiter

Jupiter gives a great deal of energy to the earth, and it is often combined with the Sun and Mars in various effects. Jupiter rules the liver, the arteries (flow of blood away from the heart), especially of the stomach (assimilation of food) and legs, fibrin in the blood (with Mars and Pisces), the spleen, the kidneys (with Venus), fatty tissues, the body's ability to fight disease, oxygen in the blood, the lungs, the right ear, sperm, and general maintenance of the body. Jupiter influences the occipital lobe of the hypophysis (pituitary body) and body growth.

Diseases of Jupiter are due to immoderation in food intake, poor digestion, weak blood, and congestion. Jupiter does not cause diseases, but excess will trigger poor aspects with other planets.

Saturn

Saturn is the planet of restriction, contraction, and limitation. It is the natural counterbalance to Jupiter's outgoing nature, and it is the planet of karma (Book of Life), or cosmic bookkeeping.

Self-discipline is required to experience the positive benefits of Saturn; otherwise, it appears negative, hostile, and punitive. Saturn guards the entrance to the invisible worlds (thirty-second path) as the "Guardian of the Threshold."

Saturn rules time, chronic diseases, the bones, the teeth, flexibility of the spine, all aging processes, the anterior lobe of the pituitary, the auditory organs (including hardening of the ear drum), the bladder, sterility, circulation (slowing down), absorption of minerals, the calves and knees, the cervical vertebrae, the vagus nerve, the spleen, and memory (long-term). Saturn is associated with rheumatism, calcifications, hardening of tissues, depression, melancholy, frigidity, lethargy, chronic conditions, and crankiness.

Using Planetary Colors and Cycles for Healing

Color therapy is one of the easiest ways of using planetary symbols and energies, for both the recipient and healer.

In addition to associating the colors with specific organs of the body, as listed above, they can also be used generally. This is most commonly done by visualizing oneself inhaling and exhaling the chosen color. Sometimes this is inhaling the color bright and exhaling it dark to symbolize a release of the chaotic energies causing the disruption, be it emotional or physical. The colors can also be breathed into and out of someone else, via visualization, to act as a kind of tuning fork for the healing process.

Colors as they are often described are used singularly, and rarely with either their planetary symbol or their complementary color, as they are in Hermetic and Kabbalistic practices. Combining the color with its symbols and complementary color adds significant focus and effectiveness to the healing process.

Using Cycles of Seven in Health and Wellness

If healing is bringing to wholeness, or, as some have suggested, a state of "holiness," then we must accept that in our world, healing takes time. Even "instantaneous" healing takes some level of measurable time, be it one second, a minute, or an hour. This "time" is a reflection of the transmission of information and energy from the invisible to the visible.

Just as the endocrine and nerve energies of the human body are the intermediary of energy between the visible and invisible worlds—that is, the etheric energy—the planets are the reflectors of etheric energy into our solar system from the Sephiroth.

1. The planets are the psychic centers, or chakras, of the solar system, and through them we get our energetic impulses.

2. By identifying an illness in relationship to a planet, we can derive the best time for giving treatments, be that the best day of the week or the best time (i.e., planetary hour) of a given day. We can also identify adverse periods as well.

3. By identifying an illness in relation to its more physical or psychological nature, we can identify the best time of treatment, the period of treatment, and the zodiacal (elemental and planetary) forces involved; in more advanced work, lunar or solar cycles should be taken into consideration.

4. By identifying a person's "solar day," or day of their birth in relation to the week (such as Friday, Monday, and so forth), we can find the best day for that person to begin activities, receive healing, and receive inspiration.

5. By identifying someone's "day of rest," or the day prior to their solar day, we can also find the day that is best for that person to finish business, reflect, and avoid starting new activities.

Planets and the Days of the Week

Each day of the week is ruled by a particular planet that influences the energies of that day, much in the same way a filter changes the appearance of light. This tincting or coloring of the day's energies in turn influences activities and events that occur during the day. By picking days most in harmony with our chosen activity—in this case, healing of a particular illness or mental-emotional condition—we increase the amount of supportive energy available to us. Known as planetary hours, these influences further divide and create a series of energy patterns that are unique to each day, thereby allowing for skilled practitioners to find the most precise time for a particular work. For our purposes, however, the general current of the day will suffice.

Day	Planet	Simple Color	Complementary Color
Saturday	Saturn	Black	White
Sunday	Sun	Golden yellow	Violet
Monday	Moon	Purple	Yellow
Tuesday	Mars	Red	Green
Wednesday	Mercury	Orange	Blue
Thursday	Jupiter	Blue	Orange
Friday	Venus	Green	Red

Below is an alternate color scheme that works just as well; it uses colors specific to the planets instead of using the colors of the Sephiroth in extension. One may choose to use both color systems: one for when working on the Sephiroth and the second for when working with the planets. This is really a personal choice and requires some experimentation on the part of each student.

Planet	Positive/ Active	Negative/ Passive
Saturn	Indigo	Black
Sun	Orange	Yellow or gold
Moon	Blue	Puce (a dark red)
Mars	Bright red	Bright red
Mercury	Yellow	Orange
Jupiter	Purple	Blue
Venus	Emerald green	Emerald green

Technique—Using Planetary Powers in Healing

Explanation—Once the elemental energies have been invoked and established, the energies of the planets can be brought into play to further refine and assist the healing process.

Type of Practice—This technique is to be used as needed. In the beginning, it should be practiced once or twice a month until all of the planets have been performed at least once to gain familiarity and confidence with the method.

Preparation—Pick the subject to be treated in advance. Be familiar with its corresponding planetary color and symbol. Perform the Middle Pillar on the day corresponding to the planet and the issue to be addressed. If possible, perform the purification practice prior to the Middle Pillar, as well as the Six Directions and the Attunement to the Tradition if time allows. However, these are not required.

Method—Once the Middle Pillar is performed, proceed as follows:

1. Visualize the color of the planet corresponding to the condition or organ to be treated as flowing into you from the Crown and down your left side, linking to the material element of earth, and flowing up your right side back to the Crown.

2. As you inhale, imagine that as the energy moves into your body, it pushes any energy blocks down and out of the body to be purified by the earth.

3. As you exhale, imagine as the energy moves up the body that it pushes any energy blocks out of the body to be dissolved and purified by Spirit.

4. Continue with this process for several minutes, filling your body and aura with a brilliant colored energy of the planet being used, and see the edge of your aura tinged in its complementary color.

5. After you have filled your aura with this brilliant energy, focus your attention on the specific area or organ to be treated. See it being filled with this unlimited supply of brilliant energy. Imagine that energy from across the universe is being drawn into your aura and body and being directed toward the successful healing of your body and mind.

6. Vibrate the divine name corresponding to the planet several times. When in doubt, use an odd number, such as three, seven, or nine.

7. If you are familiar with it, imagine the planetary symbol glowing from within the organ and bringing strength, vitality, and healthy function to it, and imagine this spreading to the rest of your aura. Use the complementary color for the planetary sign, or simply a brilliant white.

8. Continue with this for several minutes.

9. When completed, imagine the brilliant energy of your aura being pulled into the organ or area being treated, bringing health, strength, and vitality to it.

Incorporation into Daily Practice—Perform this exercise once a day, changing the color and planet to match the planetary energies of the day. This will further increase your attunement to the natural energies as well as reduce friction from astrological conditions. Do this until you are familiar with the effects and uses of each of the planets.

The planetary energies can also be used to change material conditions in our lives (concrete expressions of inner emotional states) that we want to improve. In *The Art of True Healing*, Israel Regardie outlines a simple and direct method for using the planetary energies to improve mental, emotional, physical, and material conditions.

However, instead of using complementary colors, he uses a color scheme of active and passive or positive and negative colors. Both systems appear to work equally well, and experimentation will allow individual practitioners to discover what is best for their own work. One of the advantages of Regardie's active and passive color scheme for the planets is that it helps to make a clearer distinction between the energies we are subconsciously associating with the spheres of the Tree of Life and the spheres' denser manifestation through the planets, although there is clearly some overlap.

Some of the material and psychological associations for the planets are as follows:

Sun
Material Conditions: Life, money, all forms of growth, health and happiness, leadership positions, and dealings with superiors, officials, and anyone in authority or power.
Psychological Conditions: Power and success, imagination, spiritual Illumination, and mental strength and wellness.

Moon
Material Conditions: Changes and fluctuations of all kinds, weather, short journeys, and gain and loss.

Psychological Conditions: The personality, how we are perceived by the public, relations to women, internal mood swings, and psychic perception and development.

Mercury

Material Conditions: Buying and selling of goods, all business affairs (particularly day-to-day ones), transfer of information or its reception, contracts and all manner of writing, and short travels.

Psychological Conditions: Judgment, analysis, communication and thinking, intellectual capabilities and intellectual friendships, magical and alchemical knowledge, and initiation.

Mars

Material Conditions: Surgery, physical strength and vitality, energy, muscle development and tone, male sexual power.

Psychological Conditions: Willpower, haste, anger, and all forms of construction and destruction.

Venus

Material Conditions: Art, music, theater, social activities and events, decorations, harmony of design, luxury, self-indulgence, all forms of beauty of mind, body, home, social settings, and dealings with women or younger people.

Psychological Conditions: Affections and emotions, and all forms of physical and sexual pleasure and its relation to inner happiness or conditions.

Jupiter

Material Conditions: Banks, creditors, gambling, dealing with debtors, expansion in business, social standing, and all forms of growth.

Psychological Conditions: Spirituality, philosophy, occult studies for initiation, visions, dreams, long memory, and generosity of heart, hand, and purse.

Saturn

Material Conditions: Debts and repayment, agriculture, real estate, wills, inheritance, old plans, old people, and old relationships.

Psychological Conditions: Inertia, depression, stability, and firmness.

Technique—Using Planetary Powers to Change Material Conditions

Explanation—Once the elemental energies have been invoked and established, the energies of the planets can be used to address specific material conditions.

Type of Practice—This technique is to be used as needed. In the beginning, it should be practiced until all of the planets have been performed at least once to gain familiarity and confidence with the method.

Preparation—Pick the subject to be treated in advance. Be familiar with its corresponding planetary color and symbol. Perform the Middle Pillar on the day corresponding to the planet and the issue to be addressed. If possible, perform the purification practice prior to the Middle Pillar, as well as the Six Directions and the Attunement to the Tradition if time allows. However, these are not required.

Method—Once the Middle Pillar is performed, proceed as follows:

1. Visualize the color of the planet corresponding to the condition or organ to be treated as flowing into you from the Crown and down your left side, linking to the material element of earth, and flowing up your right side back to the Crown.

2. As you inhale, imagine that as the energy moves into your body, it pushes any energy blocks down and out of the body to be purified by the earth.

3. As you exhale, imagine as the energy moves up the body that it pushes any energy blocks out of the body to be dissolved and purified by Spirit.

4. Continue with this process for several minutes, filling your body and aura with a brilliant colored energy of the planet being used, and see the edge of your aura tinged in its complementary color.

5. After you have filled your aura with this brilliant energy, focus your attention on the specific subject to be treated. See it being fulfilled and completed in a joyful and harmonious manner. Imagine that you are filled with this unlimited supply of brilliant energy and that energy

from across the universe is being drawn into your aura and body and being directed toward the successful achievement of your objective.

6. Vibrate the divine name corresponding to the planet several times. When in doubt, use an odd number, such as three, seven, or nine.

7. If you are familiar with it, imagine the planetary symbol glowing from within your heart and bringing strength, vitality, and healthy function to your entire being. Imagine this spreading to the rest of your aura. Use the complementary color for the planetary sign, or simply a brilliant white.

8. Continue with this for several minutes.

9. When completed, imagine the brilliant energy of your aura being pulled into your heart, bringing health, strength, and vitality to it, as well as a successful completion of your visualized objective.

Incorporation into Daily Practice—Start on Saturday, using the energies of Saturn to address a Saturn issue. Perform the exercise for one week, staying with the Saturn energies. This will further increase your attunement to the natural energies as well as reduce friction from astrological conditions. Do this until you are familiar with the effects and uses of each of the planets. Once done, move to solar issues, starting on Sunday, and so forth until you have used each planet for an entire week to address one specific material issue connected with it.

Using Sound, Touch, Smell, and Imagery in the Healing Process

Massage, therapeutic touch, aromatherapy, toning, music therapy, and guided visualization are not new to "integrative medicine." Each in fact has its roots in the occult traditions of Western (as well as Eastern) esotericism and in various native practices. Even homeopathy and spagyric herbal tinctures, common in Europe, are rooted in the Hermetic-alchemical tradition.

Within esotericism, the use of sound in the form of chants, smell through incense and oils, and imagery both internal and external to affect consciousness are well known. The ability to transfer part or all of this heightened state or access to increased energy was most commonly demonstrated in the form of a blessing or initiation involving physical contact. In the New Testament, we hear Jesus asking who has touched him as he passes through a crowd, stating that his "virtue" or power has gone out of him. The belief in this form of healing touch extended well into the sixteenth and seventeenth centuries in parts of Europe. It originated in the belief of the "Divine Right of Kings" to rule, and as God's representative on earth, royalty of both sexes had healing power in their hands. Many sought this form of "divine blessing" to heal illness, and when the practice was curtailed, popular demand often brought it back.

It is quite easy to combine all of these tools—sound, smell, touch, and imagery—into a single synthetic healing technique by using the Doctrine of Correspondences. For example, a person complaining of lung problems can be told to imagine bright blue and orange energy entering the lungs while inhaling, and dark, dirty energy leaving upon exhaling. After a few minutes of this, the person can just focus on the idea of inhaling and exhaling a bright blue energy with orange highlights. While doing this, the person can also visualize the symbol for Jupiter, its seal, or any number of Jupiter-associated images. Simple is best, though. Incense or essential oils can be burned or evaporated pertaining to Jupiter. In instances in which there is actual therapeutic benefit from the oil (such as eucalyptus) and a relation to the planet, this is best.

If the person receiving the treatment is being assisted by a practicing healer, the healer can stand behind the person, hand on the shoulder, close to the spine, thumbs touching the sides of the spine if possible, and perform the same breathing and visualization as the recipient. However, practitioners will imagine themselves as inhaling the energy and it going through them into the recipient. When they exhale, they will imagine the dark energy moving out of the patient. It is best if the breathing of the practitioner and recipient can be harmonized, although this will happen naturally. This can also be done by sitting across from the person, sitting close to avoid strain, and holding hands as the breathing and visualization take place.

Methods of Energy Transfer through Physical Mediums

Nature provides us with a great deal of energy available through physical mediums, many of which we use as food. However, this is often just enough for daily living, and it does not provide us with sufficient reserves for psychic health as well. Just as Kabbalists have demonstrated that energy can be focused and stored in talismans (solid material objects), alchemists have demonstrated that energy can be released from material objects.

Herbal tinctures are a perfect example of this, as are genuine alchemical products. Even a simple product such as wine, common in sacramental rites, is traditionally seen as a stimulant in small doses and holds a great deal of energy, which is transferred via its alcohol content. Red wine is the preferred medium, and it is not surprising that this is also rich in antioxidants, a known aging retardant. Taken in this light, the Christian rite of Holy Communion, derived from the ancient rite of Melkazadik, and beyond, is a true act of talismanic magic and alchemy combined.

Water, blood, and sexual fluids—even feces, urine, and saliva—have at times been used as mediums for transferring psychic or, more accurately, etheric energy in healing, initiatic, and general esoteric activities. We see Jesus mixing his spit with clay to heal a blind man. Blood sacrifices (holocaust) were performed among all of the ancient temples at some point in time.

A modern form of "energetic healing" that is a blend of sympathetic and talismanic magic, with a modern technological appearance, is radionics. Here, boxes made of cardboard and wire are used to direct healing energy at a person by using a single hair or a personal possession from the individual. When understood in the light of psychology, it is clear that patients are "healing themselves" through auto-suggestion. In the light of esotericism, auto-suggestion, coupled with the energetic transfer from the director of the device, is the means of healing. This is simply an explanation of radionics; all forms of healing must be weighed against their successes—and not how or why they work—if they are to be judged as successful and useful.

Energy Accumulation, Storage, and Transfer: The Magic of Water

Just as fire is the most significant element for the development and expansion of consciousness, earth for the materialization of our desired outcomes, and air for binding the universe together and transmitting ideas and energy between the spiritual and emotional worlds, water is the key to transferring energy between the visible and invisible worlds.

Exercise—Charging Water

Explanation—Charging water is a wonderful way of practicing one's ability to direct energy as well as to test its efficiency. Charged water can be used on plants, given to pets, consumed, or even used to assist someone in need of treatment who might not otherwise be able to respond well to more interactive methods, as it not only strengthens the aura, but also imparts energy at a highly absorbable level directly into the cells through digestion. Charged water also tends to taste slightly different and demonstrate greater surface tension. This is one of the most practical and beneficial exercises presented.

Type of Practice—This is an exercise that should be practiced often and utilized during healing treatments.

Preparation—Prepare in any way of your choosing.

Method—After you have prepared, begin as follows:

1. Hold a glass of cold water between both hands, approximately six to twelve inches from your solar plexus. If necessary, the glass can be placed on a table, as long as your hands are around the rim and near the top of the water.

2. Breathe slowly and deeply. Feel warmth grow in your solar plexus, and imagine that a brilliant stream of bluish-white energy is flowing from there through your arms and into the water. Continue with this for several minutes.

3. When you are done, drink the water, and then meditate for a few minutes.

It is important that the glass be about six to twelve inches away from your solar plexus in order to act as a magnet to draw out your psychic body and thereby expand your aura. Doing this before going to sleep will assist in the healing process, as well as dreaming and astral projection. In this instance, the water can be reduced to a few ounces to avoid excessive urination during the evening, or you can leave it near the bedside on level with the head, and if possible to the left side.

Incorporation into Daily Practice—This exercise has many uses and should be incorporated into the weekly practice of anyone dealing with energetic healing on a regular basis or those wishing to strengthen their psychic body. After a week or two of practice, it need not be done every day, as several times a week will suffice. Once you have developed skill, practice charging the water with the elements and planetary energies, as well as holding the glass while circulating the energies as described in previous exercises.

Exercise—Healing Roses

Explanation—This exercise demonstrates the development of healing abilities.

Type of Practice—Exercise.

Preparation—Select a method of preparation from the previous exercises and practices.

Method—After you have prepared, proceed as follows:
1. Obtain two or three small roses from a florist.
2. Place each one in a small vase or glass with fresh water. One rose should have nutritional additive in the water to extend its life span. This powdered additive is often supplied when flowers are purchased. Place the remaining two roses in plain water, either tap or bottled, but be sure to use the same water source for all three roses. Label the first rose A to distinguish it from the others, and label one of the two remaining roses B.
3. Place them near each other so that they can be examined as a group.

4. Once a day, take the rose labeled B and either place it on the table before you or hold it before your solar plexus as you did with the water exercise above. Be sure to be at least three to six feet away from the other roses when doing this.

5. Energize the rose for three to five minutes. Let it sit where it is for several minutes, and then return it to the row where the remaining roses are.

6. Over the course of a week or more, notice which roses wilt and die first. If done properly, the charged rose will outlive the noncharged and nutritionally supplemented roses.

Incorporation into Daily Practice—This exercise should be done occasionally as a means of assessing your healing skills.

The Red and White Stones of the Alchemists and How They Are Used

Alchemy is often called the "Royal Art" and is considered to be the pinnacle of Hermetic practices. Its goal is to perfect the human personality through a series of chemical and metallurgical operations that if successfully completed are seen as a material demonstration of an achieved interior state. Like the *siddhas* of yoga or the *charismen* of the New Testament, various abilities at "transmutation" become available to adepts as they climb the Hermetic ladder. Among the best known of these abilities is the power to transmute one metal or mineral into another; the ability to cure disease; the creation of a universal cure, or *panacea*; and the ability to live a long life, nearing immortality by human standards, through creation of the *Elixir Vitae*.

In summary, we can say that these spiritually medicinal products called Elixirs and Stones can be simply defined as the greatest concentration of etheric life force or energy in the smallest amount of liquid (Elixir) or matter (Stone). These medicines are created through a thorough understanding of the Kabbalistic chain of correspondences, maximized though the use of cyclic pulses and energetic patterns as represented in astrology, and made with the methods of "solve et coagula" as demonstrated by alchemy.

In an article on alchemy, Rosicrucian and Freemason Francis Mayer[1] writes:

Now in alchemy, the zodiac and the planets are considered as located in the organism of man, including the auric bodies, the vital [etheric], sidereal [astral], even the solar [Body of Light] bodies. In consequence of this duplicity, i.e., physical and hyper-physical, of our organism complicated by the fact that it functions on four planes [Four Worlds], the ancients were reticent and left it to the initiator to reveal the exact locations of starts and planets in the body, because it could be understood by the practitioner only, who is familiar with hyper-physical organisms and planes of consciousness. Moreover, they knew by experience that unskilled handling of this delicate and complicated machinery may cause transitory or even permanent malfunctional disorders.

And further on:

So while it is still difficult to find the exact actual locations, it has become an open secret that the planets and the zodiac of the sun as well as of the moon are centered in or around the brain, the spine, the glands and the diverse plexus. Also that these organs are in more or less constant and intense intercommunication with the circumambient aether. Consequently, the seven circulations and following imbibitions by which the white and red elixirs are produced, mean in plain English but circulations of our vital energy, our fixed power, through different plexus and glands, also brain and spine, as well as the reinforcing of this energy by imbibitions from the circumambient aether, our volatile mercury, which by the operation is drawn in, becomes assimilated, coagulated and fixed in our organism.

In mineral alchemy, the White Stone works on healing the body, opening up the astral worlds, and giving a medicine that seems to heal all ills. The Red Stone, created through the same process as the White, only more demanding, gives access to the powers of the heart and, with it, all levels of matter, energy, and consciousness in an integrated fashion. However, this is not the end. Even after the Red Stone is made, it still must be "multiplied"

1 Francis Mayer, a thirty-second-degree Mason and ninth-degree member of the Societas Rosicruciana in America (SRIA), was an important figure in the early years of the movement, penning many articles for the organization's publication, *Mercury*. Mayer was cared for by the society in his later years, and on his death was interned near society luminaries, including Plummer, Theodotus, and Serena. The excerpts presented here are from one of Mayer's more important articles that was made available to members of the Rosicrucian Order in AMORC's Rose-Croix University classes on alchemy in the mid 1940s. It was originally published in two parts in March and June 1928. Special thanks to Maria Babwahsingh, imperatrix of the SRIA, for providing permission to quote this information.

or pushed up further levels on the Tree of Life until it and its creator are on the edge of the final step on the Path of Return.

It is interesting to note that red is the color of the alchemist's robes and those of the magus in many traditional works of art as well as in modern tarot decks. Red is also the color of victory, success, divine blessing, and the energy of the Original Being (Adam). People who wear red are often more successful and feel more confident in their actions. In traditional Kabbalah, red strings were given as a means of keeping evil away. If a special robe, tunic, or piece of clothing were to be worn during healing work, red in one or more of its shades would be an appropriate color to pick.

Notes on Self

1. The Ruach, or self, can be thought of as the ego, be it in a primitive or well-developed state. This sense of self that we have, as autonomous beings interacting in the world and with other beings, is the nucleus around which we build our lives. In its perfect state, "it" or "we" are aware of our relationship and control over the unconscious forces of the Nephesh (subconscious/etheric) and Guph (etheric/physical body), as well as open to and even subservient to the influx of energies, inspiration, and knowledge of the Neshamah, or "Higher Self." The Ruach is in reality a projection of the Neshamah, just as the *persona*, or personality, is a projection of the Ruach.

2. *Persona* is the mask we wear in different social and interpersonal situations. We may even identify with it so much as to believe it to be our "true self." This is identical to the persona who is overly nationalistic or who is concerned with a "role," such as "father, mother, child, business person, cleric, healer, spiritual guide," and so forth. Psychosynthesis states that we have one main personality (Tiphareth projected into Yesod) and several sub-personalities (the remaining Sephiroth as they are projected into Yesod).

3. The persona is a tool that allows us to interact with other individuals in the world; that is what it is for, and that is the extent of its true use.

4. Higher Self, Neshamah, the spark, the only part that can truly say "I am"—this is what we experience for fleeting moments between sleep and wakefulness, when we are no longer aware of the body, who we "are," or our daily concerns. It exists in potential as a force in the mundane world, but only if the ego and persona are in harmony and agree to become open to its influences.

5. *Character* is who we are—what we carry with us from incarnation to incarnation, that is consistent regardless of our persona, how we act in our dreams as well as waking state. It is our mark of integration of the Self, ego, and personality. Character is defined by our habits. A *habit* is a conscious act done repeatedly to the point at which it becomes unconscious.

Notes on Solar Centers

1. The solar plexus (and at times the navel), heart, and cerebrum (front of brain) all work in a "solar" or active fashion. These also correspond to the three cauldrons of Chinese inner alchemy. The Emerald Tablet speaks of completing the work of the Sun, as the Sun is the giver of life, symbolized by Venus; as such, it is also known as "the Lord of the Two Worlds" (inner and outer). This is why the awakening of Tiphareth is so important: it allows us greater access and exchange between the visible and invisible worlds.

2. The Moon is the gate, Mercury unites, the Sun rules, and Venus is the expression.

3. When meditating on the solar plexus (or even the navel, although this energy is greatly more physical in nature), we can add the idea and feeling that this meditation is harmonizing the etheric and emotional (astral) energies of our Nephesh (higher and lower Nephesh, unconscious).

4. When meditating on the heart, we can add the feeling that this is harmonizing the energies of our unconscious (Nephesh) and consciousness (Ruach).

5. When meditating on our pituitary, we can feel that this is harmonizing the energies between our spiritual consciousness (Neshamah) and our sense of self (Ruach).

6. Of course, the idea need also be strongly formulated that these spiritual energies flow though us and are harmonized with our unconscious and physical bodies, not somehow limited to our brains or a mental state.

7. Dion Fortune states in *The Circuit of Force* that nearly all illnesses find their seat below the diaphragm, and for that reason it is important to keep the solar plexus in good repair and to use it in making treatments. The reason for this is simple. Not only is the solar plexus a central tuning note as a whole for the physical and psychic bodies, it is also the physical body's central source of radiating etheric and psychic energy, after the hands, feet, and eyes. The body is continually radiating energy, but for lack of a central focus (i.e., a strong solar plexus), those around us are not aware of it.

Key Points

- The four elements, four bodies, and four areas of consciousness relate to the four forces of modern physics.

- The etheric energy the elements represent concentrates in specific areas of the human body, as well as spheres in the Tree of Life as it relates to the material universe.

- The seven ancient planets are the dense etheric and material expression of the energy radiated by the spheres of the Tree of Life. They are a specific expression of that energy and should not be confused with the broader, more general energy-intelligence of the spheres.

- Kether provides the energy for the Tree to be; Tiphareth harmonizes its various expressions; Yesod personalizes it; and Malkuth expresses it completely and fully.

- The planets relate to organs and functions of the body and can be used to heal those organs and actions of the body through direct energy work, plant tinctures, mineral extractions, and ritualistic operations.

- Energy can be transferred to others in various mediums, of which liquids are the easiest and most efficient if charging is required. Water and wine are the most common forms of energy transfer.

- To correctly understand anatomical correspondences, as they can often be duplicated, it is important to understand the function of the planet, as well as the organ, and how on a practical level the energy-intelligence-organ interface will be expressed.

Assignments for Chapter 6

1. Perform the exercises in this chapter, paying careful attention to your experiences and recording them in your notebook. Spend at least one week each on the Charging Water and Healing Roses exercises. These are simple practices that can deliver profound results, and they should not be underestimated.

2. Meditate on the definitions of the Red and White Stone, as well as a Stone and an Elixir, as given in this chapter. How do they correspond to your physical body?

3. Identify the planetary color scheme for your work and begin integrating it into your association of the planets, their powers, the day of the week, and the areas of the body they affect.

Chapter 7

The Crucible of the Heart:
Inner Alchemy and Kabbalah

Chapter Overview
- *The Purifying Fire in Alchemy and Kabbalah*
- *How to Attune to the Inner Teacher*
- *Morality and Ethics in Esotericism and Healing*

The Purifying Fire in Alchemy and Kabbalah

It is impossible to understand alchemical phenomena without making reference to the tradition, in particular, the *Aesh Metzareth*, or "Purifying Fire," an alchemical-Kabbalistic text of Jewish origin. As we have seen, the tradition states that the universe is composed of ten levels of energy condensation, with each level being harmonious with the others but possessing its own unique characteristics of matter, consciousness, and energy. This primordial energy flows continually throughout creation, always following the same path, and condenses to form the material world. Each aspect of matter in turn reflects a higher plane above it, and fixes some of that plane's unique

"To practice the middle way it is indispensable to know the powers of the heart, since its influence must predominate. This Way is a continual balance between the egoism of the Personal Self and the altruism of the Spiritual Self. Only the heart can achieve this wonderful balance, by its mediating position between the temporal and the extratemporal, between the moral organism and its immortal archetype."

Schwaller de Lubize,
Opening of the Way

energy in the material world. Thus, gold relates to the sun, as does the human heart, giving all three similar characteristics and an energetic relationship. Similar relationships exist throughout the material world.

Each level also has its own sublevels, and from this the tradition gives us four possible Trees of Life, all interacting and relating to one another, but each showing how matter, energy, and consciousness function in a specific way. Each of these planes we call worlds (*Olam*), and each has its own affinity to one of the elements of earth, water, air, or fire. From this, we can then reduce the number of Trees to one, but we also show each sphere as having four sublevels, each relating to one of the elements.

Of all the elements, fire is the most important, as it gives life and consciousness to matter. It is fire that removes spiritual impurities and prepares us for initiation. Many systems, particularly alchemy, speak of the Secret Fire and its liberation from matter. When this is done, when the fire energy of the material world—or, more accurately, our physical body—is liberated, it climbs the Tree of Life, reuniting itself with the fire element of each of the individual spheres. This gives rise to consciousness on all levels and is the Kabbalistic understanding of the phenomenon of kundalini.

The Teacher

In traditional esoteric studies, a student would either be associated with a teacher for a long period of time or undergo a series of initiations in a structured setting; between these initiations, instruction would be given by a series of teachers specializing in particular areas.

With the breakdown of traditional teaching practices, the rarity of qualified instructors, and the lack of operating lodges for initiatic instruction, students must go from class to class, center to center, and seminar to seminar, attempting to gather enough information to move forward on their Path. From these experiences, they cobble together their own vision of "the Teacher" and hope someday to find him or her in the flesh. This is in some ways no different than what occurred in the Eastern schools, where students would travel for years before settling on one person as their teacher to guide them on the Path.

While the idea of a single all-knowing, perfect teacher is enticing, it is for the most part an infantile fantasy born of unresolved Freudian issues. Even in Eastern schools, where the teacher is looked upon as an enlightened being capable of doing no wrong, it is still understood that this may not be the case, and a certain amount of leeway is given in personal areas. The personality of the teacher is put aside, pending grievous misconduct, and the quality of the teaching is what is considered.

When we look at the idea of the teacher in Western esotericism, we see a great deal of discussion on the topics of the Inner Teacher, the Inner Master, the Holy Guardian Angel, and similar terms. This Inner Master is none other than our own enlightened consciousness. When we first encounter it, this aspect of our psyche often appears as a separate individual, because while it is always present, we are not always aware of it. As such, we are "separate" from it in our daily life. When the Great Awakening occurs (often called the "alchemical marriage"), we "unite" with this function, and two become one. We still function as an individual in the world, but we are aware of our fundamental unity with others and creation.

All authentic spiritual teachers are attempting to stimulate this inner awakening in us in some manner. They act as a reflection of what is possible for us, of what we are becoming and growing into. However, not all teachers are "fully Illuminated," and therefore they are limited in what they can pass on, just as students are limited in what they can learn due to their own weaknesses and failings.

Modern students are demanding and immature in their attitude toward spiritual work. Fantasies of instant attainment fill their heads, and the basic role of ethical and moral teachings, coupled with the work of memorizing rituals, scriptures, prayers, and traditional languages and words, does not interest them. Many even see it as an obstacle to the Path. In short, they seek to have what they want when they want it, and they do not feel any obligation to their teacher, community, or the tradition—they have paid their entrance fees and that is sufficient.

Such attitudes, while prevalent, are an obstacle to true attainment, as the tradition cannot be written in a book and sold. That is just the seeds. The true plant and its fruit—Illumination—are won only by diligent work and a humbling of the self before the Light of the Master, be it within or without.

If you are not willing to do scales, then you will not be able to learn to play a musical instrument. If you are not willing to draw endless circles and squares, then the subtleties of fine drawing will never be yours. If you are not willing to be still, listen, follow advice, and discipline yourself in your practice, then the desire for magical powers, Illumination, or the ability to heal are just egotistical pipe dreams or, worse, fantasies that keep you from living a meaningful life in the world, even if it is not a very spiritual one.

It is important that we adopt the proper attitude toward our self and our studies, toward life, and toward our teachers and the tradition.

This attitude can be summed up in one word—gratitude.

If we are to awaken to our Inner Master, then we must find five physical teachers to stimulate our inner awakening. Each teacher represents a reflection of the Inner Master, and as such, we can look upon each of our teachers as a specific incarnation or embodiment of that particular skill and ideal. By doing this, we save ourselves and our teachers the burden of projection and psychological wish fulfillment so common in today's spiritual marketplace. Since no one person is seen as "perfect" and as being there solely to help us—or, more likely in the pathological sense, meet our emotional and psychological needs—we reduce the risk of having unpleasant associations.

It is important, however, that we have someone whom we look to as embodying the totality of the tradition and who has demonstrated genuine gifts and inspired teachings, even if we do not look at this teacher as being a "Perfect Master" or some such thing. We simply need to recognize the important place and role this person has played for us in our spiritual growth and with assistance in the Path of Becoming. This is our primary teacher, who will hold a special place in our heart as well as our prayers and meditations.

We then need teachers who embody the practical expression of the elements as they relate to the tradition. No title need be given them, although it is easy to see how they can be assigned. For example, someone who is an expert in ritual, conveys its importance, and instructs us in it in a special and memorable manner could be the Master of Ceremonies or the Master of Ritual. This is the earth element of the tradition.

There are also the devotional and psychic aspects of the work. This person demonstrates to us the power of emotions, spiritual devotion, and prayer in our desire to grow. This is the Master of Arts, for devotions often express themselves artistically through music, poetry, song, crafts, writing, and visual formats. This is the water element of the tradition.

Thirdly, we have the intellectual and academic training needed to train the mind to think clearly and reason properly along proper channels, so as to come to useful and meaningful conclusions. This is the Master of the Teachings, the air element of the tradition.

Fourth, there is the inspirational teacher, who reveals in often dangerous and no uncertain terms the nature of our work. Each of the previous teachers corrects us, often gently so as not to bruise our fragile ego, whereas this master burns away our illusions and, in his or her mercy, holds nothing back. This is the Master of Illumination, the Master of Initiation, and is the fire element of the tradition.

Our primary teacher embodies a part of all of these and, as such, is the Spirit or unifying aspect of the tradition as far as our personal work is concerned.

If we bring the proper attitude to these teachers, then they will stimulate their corresponding element in us and we will be prepared for the arrival of the Perfect Master, the Inner Master, which is nothing other than our own Illuminated consciousness.

Exercise—Practice of Spiritual Gratitude

1. Imagine your primary teacher before you and give heartfelt thanks for this teacher's stimulating the spiritual current within you and starting you on this Path.

2. Do the same for the Master of Ceremonies or Rituals, for giving you proper guidance on the importance of ceremony, form, structure, and tradition.

3. Do the same for the Master of Devotion, for showing you how to take the material form and bring it to life.

4. Then do the same for the Master of Teaching, for showing you how all is connected and necessary and that the mind is the source of all Being.

5. Finally, thank the Master of Illumination, for fearlessly burning away your iniquities, weaknesses, and faults and introducing you to the power of Being.

6. See them all together, merging into a sphere of golden light, and bask in that light for a while.

Exercise—Awakening the Inner Master

There are many variations on this exercise, with their common theme being that of "awakening." The symbol of the sleeping Venus that cannot be seen with mortal eyes survives in the story of Sleeping Beauty. The resurrection of the master is present in many ancient myths and initiation rituals. In Kabbalah and alchemy, many of these stories are often accompanied by a sound such as a trumpet or horn, by a book or scroll, or sometimes by both, announcing the arrival of an angelic messenger. Mary is approached by Gabriel, the archangel of the Annunciation. When John is on the Island of Patmos and has his visions, better known as Revelations or the Apocalypse, they are accompanied by the sounds of trumpets. Christian Rosenkreutz is visited by an angel in the opening pages of the *Alchemical Wedding of Christian Rosenkreutz*. Even Nicholas Flamel is visited by an angelic messenger carrying a strange book prior to his purchase of the now-famous Hieroglyphs of Abraham the Jew, the book that led him on his journey to the perfection of the Philosopher's Stone.

This awakening must be thought of as gradual. Just as we awaken from a night's sleep to the light of day in stages, so do we awaken to our inner light of day, or the "Golden Dawn" ("Red Morning" of Jakob Boehme), in phases. In many respects, every exercise in *Kabbalah for Health & Wellness* will assist you in awakening your awareness of self; the exercises will also do the same for others on whom they might be used for physical and emotional healing. However, it is only through a clear and dedicated devotion to this task that we can really hope to experience this new inner life. Psychic talents can be developed and experiences of inner worlds had, but only by making each day a dedication to our inner life, and each act a reminder of our heartfelt desire to experience the true quintessential experience of inner truth, can we be said to be on "the Path."

Since each person will have different inclinations based on previous experience, this book gives several methods to stimulate this awakening. Spend about four weeks with each one to allow the full lunar effects to be stimulated. Pay attention to your results, and after you have completed at least one round (two or three would be better), find the practice that gives you the best outcome and stick with it.

The Healing Power of Forgiveness

Forgiving is not forgetting; it is learning and moving on. Let go of perceived or actual offenses committed by others against you in their fear and ignorance. Reminding yourself of them only distracts you from living now and damages your road into the future. Put them behind you. Start with the small things and move on to the larger ones. Practice generating compassion (not pity) and a sincere heartfelt generosity, feeling that all who have injured you may find inner peace and that you may understand and learn from the experience. By learning from the experience, we remember it in a meaningful and useful context while no longer allowing the emotions of pain to ensnare us.

The Tetragrammaton and the Symbols of the Soul

It is often stated that true inner wholeness occurs when we awaken to our heart and experience "Knowledge and Conversation with the Holy Guardian Angel." While this is a genuine prerequisite for inner growth, and most practicing Kabbalists aspire to it, many often do not know how or where to begin. Simply telling someone to pray earnestly and devotedly is nice, but if the experiences or guidance are not in place to turn suggestion into practical action, then it is useless advice. The following meditations are designed to help the sincere student experience this inner awakening:

Permutations of the Divine Name

There are several ways to derive the appropriate permutation of the Tetragrammaton for use in experiencing inner awakening. Each is based on a different understanding of the name and its relation to the cosmos; however, they are similar enough in purpose to still be effective. The first method is based on the date of birth: simply use the name that corresponds to your astrological sign. The problem with this method is that there are several different attributions, each with its own justification for claiming authenticity. The second method is to vibrate each of the names slowly and methodically and see which name creates the greatest heart resonance. This name, then, is the one to use. There are several lists of which names are attributed to which signs and their corresponding Tribes of Israel, or Disciples of Jesus. The following version is taken from *Self-Initiation into the Golden Dawn Tradition* by Chic and Sandra Tabatha Cicero[1] and corrects two errors commonly repeated in other sources:

Aries	Taurus	Gemini	Cancer
YHVH	YHHV	YVHH	HVHY

Leo	Virgo	Libra	Scorpio
HVYH	HHYV	VHYH	VHYH

Sagittarius	Capricorn	Aquarius	Pisces
VYHH	HYHV	HYVH	HHVY

The Seventy-two Angels of the Shem ha-Mephoresh

Similar to the method using the permutations of the divine name, the seventy-two angels of the Shem ha-Mephoresh have astrological correspondences. Simply find the angel that corresponds to the period of your birth, locate its sigil, and you have the basic information needed for your meditations. The only glitch with this system is that depending on what perspective is being emphasized, some schools will start the rotation of the angels at the spring equinox, and others will start with the summer solstice. Here again, you can spend some time meditating with each name and its sigil to

---

1 Chic Cicero and Sandra Tabatha Cicero, *Self-Initiation into the Golden Dawn Tradition* (St. Paul, MN: Llewellyn, 1995), 199.

see which creates the best inner resonance, or you can use the method of vibrating the names to see which strikes you as most pertinent.

These names are not the name of your Holy Guardian Angel, but are a meaningful substitute, a key to the experience. You may find that after a period of time a new name is given to you in meditation, in a dream, or simply spontaneously. Carefully write the name down, as well as the date and time received, and spend some time with it. Tell no one the name, and do not discuss it in any manner. This is a private affair, and indiscretion can weaken or sever the fragile link you have established.

If you choose to do this meditation during the day, meditate from the heart; at night, when falling asleep, use the nape of the neck. A complete list of the angels, their sigils, and their astrological correspondences can be found in *The Kabbalah of the Golden Dawn*, by Pat Zalewski (Llewellyn). A complete listing of the angels along with their corresponding Goetic Spirits can be found in *Angels, Demons & Gods of the New Millennium*, by Lon Milo Duquette (Weiser). A word of caution, however: Goetic Spirits are very powerful and dense spirits close to the material world. They are often used to represent repressed and instinctual areas of our psyche. Working with them is extremely dangerous if you are unfamiliar with magic.

Ethics and Modern Esotericism

Ethics play a critical role in spiritual development. Unfortunately, in recent years the notion of ethics and morality has been all but lost on many who would profess to be a student of Kabbalah. This is in part due to the separation of Kabbalah from its root source—Judaism—and the creation of a modern form of eclectic Kabbalah that is being seen more as a technology for experiencing various states of consciousness, or as a kind of "positive thinking" on steroids, rather than a system of self-exploration and Becoming.

This attempt at separation is tragically flawed and ignores the fundamental keys that Kabbalah and Hermeticism give us for experiencing heightened states of awareness and gaining greater mastery over our material lives. Kabbalah is more than psychology; it is about the very essence of our being—an essence displayed through our thoughts, words, and deeds. If our conduct is not in harmony with the cosmos, then our spiritual and healing practices will be diminished. In Hermetic Kabbalah, the principal guides for ethical conduct are as follows:

1. The Ten Commandments

2. The Seven Virtues and Vices of Human Conduct

3. The Two Commandments of Jesus

The Ten Commandments

It is no surprise that there are ten spheres to the Tree of Life and Ten Commandments, giving us a definite relationship between them. While our understanding of the Ten Commandments, or "Guiding Principles," as they are referred to in Judaism, cannot be identical to how they were understood when they were given, as the culture and times are different, they are still important guides for us in assessing our conduct.

Kether = I am the Lord thy God . . .

Hokmah = Thou shalt not make graven images of me . . .

Binah = Thou shalt not take the Name of the Lord thy God in vain . . .

Chesed = Thou shalt keep holy the Sabbath . . .

Geburah = Thou shalt honor thy father and thy mother . . .

Tiphareth = Thou shalt not kill . . .

Netzach = Thou shalt not commit adultery . . .

Hod = Thou shalt not steal . . .

Yesod = Thou shalt not bear false witness against thy neighbor . . .

Malkuth = Thou shalt not covet the wife or possessions of thy neighbor . . .

If you have completed the material in this book up to this point, then you will be fully capable of creating a meditation based on the Ten Commandments and their relation to the Tree of Life and finding a means of integrating them into your spiritual life, mundane affairs, and healing work.

The Seven Virtues and Vices

Each of the seven ancient planets is given a virtue and a vice, which must be addressed as we pass through its influence either in our horoscope or through esoteric practices. These virtues and vices represent the energetic expression of the power of the planet in daily life, either as a positive and constructive force or as a negative and destructive one. There is also an additional eighth virtue and vice attributed to the planet Earth. This is the force of inertia, or laziness, which must be overcome if we are to progress in any activity, more so if it is to be a spiritual one. The virtue of Malkuth is discrimination, or the ability to make proper choices that assist one on the Path of Return.

Sphere	Virtue	Vice
Binah	Silence	Avarice
Chesed	Obedience (to Divine Law)	Hypocrisy★
Geburah	Energy/ Courage	Cruelty/ Destruction
Tiphareth	Devotion to the Great Work	Pride
Netzach	Unselfishness	Lust/ Unchastity
Hod	Truthfulness	Falsehood/ Dishonesty
Yesod	Independence	Idleness

★ Chesed is given four vices: hypocrisy, gluttony, tyranny, and bigotry, as aspects of Chesed's mercy being inverted.

The Two Commandments

These are "Love the Lord your God with all your heart and all your soul" and "Love your neighbor as yourself."

Herein is the summation of esotericism, in both seed and fruit.

The Fruit and the Method

Each sphere has a virtue and vice associated with it. The virtues offer us the fruit and the method. If we have fully developed our understanding of a sphere, then its virtue will be active in our life: that is the fruit. Yet, if we only study the sphere intellectually or attempt to use its energies in a practical manner without concern for this relation to the whole, we have failed to put into practice the very virtue that will open the sphere to us.

The vices and virtues are assigned to each of the spheres from King-dom (Malkuth) to Intelligence (Binah), with only Wisdom (Hokmah) and the Crown (Kether) being free of vice. A careful study of the virtues will also give us keys to the emotional healing needed for individuals suffering from illness related to the various spheres. As such, if someone is suffering from kidney disorders associated with purification, the planet Venus, and the sphere of Victory (Netzach), efforts should be directed at better expressing the virtue chastity, or mental and emotional purity in the form of uplifting and noble ideals, and a careful and conscientious effort should be made to limit the expression of lust and excessive attrac-tion to physical beauty alone.

The same applies to each of the remaining spheres.

While this may sound too preachy and too much like "old-time reli-gion" to many, it is in fact a critical aspect of the Path. It cannot be ignored without great risk, any more than ethics and morality can be avoided in Buddhism.

Kabbalah, alchemy, and astrology are all very systematic, abstract, and intellectual in their processing of human experience, but they are not tech-nologies like a computer or cell phone that you can simply punch keys on and activate without personal considerations. They are more like organ-isms in biotechnology, or living entities that have both specific functions and the ability to adapt and respond to their environment—in this case, the consciousness of the operator.

We can spend our entire life performing Kabbalistic rituals, making and consuming spagyric tinctures, and studying astrological charts in our search for deeper meaning, but if we do not address our emotional defi-cits and purify them, we will fail on the Path of Becoming.

Exercise—Extracting the Essence: Purification of the Centers

This exercise can be done in several manners, and as such, we will give a basic and an advanced practice. It is simply a matter of choice as to which one you perform, as both are equally effective. To be a healer means to first heal one's self of the inner knots and loci of emotional negativity associated with the limited and fearful thinking of the ego. A healer is capable of healing only up to his or her own inner level of integration. That is why some healers seem to have specialties, others are more general, and some, like Jesus, are exceptional and capable even of raising the dead.

Explanation—This practice allows you to heal your own emotional, psychological, and physical illnesses by recognizing the interconnectedness of all things. Incongruities often held deep below the level of consciousness are brought forth and integrated through the healing power of the heart.

Type of Practice—This is a core practice and is foundational to all advanced healing work.

Preparation—Prepare in any manner you choose.

Method—After you have prepared, proceed as follows:

Version One

1. Inhale, relax, and exhale, focusing on your heart (or slightly below it at the sternum) as done in previous exercises. Hold your hands either in a position of prayer or folded over your heart.

2. Pay attention to your heartbeat. Slow it down.

3. Imagine your heart as radiating a brilliant golden sphere of light and warmth, creating an invisible sphere of heat and energy around you. With practice, feel it expand to include your room, house, and beyond, extending to the ends of the universe.

4. Imagine in the center of this sphere of golden light the symbol of the Sun in violet light.

5. Focus on the virtue associated with Tiphareth, the Sun: devotion to the Great Work. Allow this to develop within you. Feel your dedication to your Becoming expand and fill your heart, radiating outward. Rest in this feeling.

6. Now, meditate on the vice of Tiphareth: pride, particularly spiritual pride, the thing that separates us from others and ourselves.

7. Remember a time when you were prideful. Pay close attention to the "small" episodes of pride, as they are the most insidious and dangerous. Remember the circumstances and how it made you feel. Take this feeling and offer it up as a sacrifice to the Great Work.

8. Imagine the feeling of pride as a dark and murky energy. It can be any color you wish, or simply a muddy and dirty yellow or gold.

9. Inhale and pull this murky color into your heart. Hold it there and feel the heat and warmth of your inner being purify this energy.

10. Exhale and feel your sphere of light expand and grow bright, and feel your devotion to the Great Work grow stronger. As you continue to inhale this energy, feel its coarse energy being released and refined inside you. Know that even in these negative habits and energies lie the seeds of your Becoming.

11. Continue with this for several minutes. Then, rest in the energy of devotion. When you are done, slowly come out of your meditation, carrying with you this feeling for as long as possible.

12. Reinvoke it across the day to reinforce it. Each time, feel a sense of pride coming over you.

13. Offer a prayer of thanks and gratitude for your success in this work and the healing it has brought to yourself and others so that you and they may experience Illumination and be a servant and friend of humanity.

Version Two: Extracting the Essence

This exercise is identical to the previous one, except that you take it an extra step and it utilizes additional energies and emotional qualities. In doing these exercises, we realize that even our self-defeating, ego-maintaining, and destructive habits can be utilized for our growth, and we realize that, in fact, that is their only purpose for being.

1. Perform steps 1 through 12 from Version One.

2. Pick a physical organ that has been giving you trouble, such as with aches and pains, or is otherwise ill. If it is not one of the seven organs listed previously in chapter 6, locate its planetary essence using correspondences. For example, bones, teeth, and hair would be Saturn; skin would be Venus. For the sense organs of perception in the head, the correspondences of the *Sepher Yetzirah* can be used.

3. See the organ filled with a dark and heavy energy that is sticky and syrupy. Breathe in and pull that energy from the organ to your heart. Think of the vice associated with the planet, and return its virtue on the out breath.

4. Feel the energies (the fire), love, and compassion of your heart purify this vice energy, and, as you exhale, send to the organ a brilliant pure-colored energy of its ruling planet, filled with its virtue.

5. As you hold your breath out, feel this energy fill the organ and radiate out from it.

6. Do this for several minutes.

7. Finally, breathe in the brilliant colored energy from the universe. Let it fill your heart and radiate out through your whole being. Do this several times, and then rest in the feeling of wholeness and wellness. Offer a prayer of thanks and gratitude for your success in this work and the healing it has brought to yourself and others so that you and they may experience Illumination and be a servant and friend of humanity.

Incorporation into Daily Practice—This practice should be performed often, as it is a synthesis of the various practices put forth in this book.

Extracting the Essence for Others

After centering yourself, perform steps 1 through 4 as in Version One and generate a profound sense of compassion and desire that the person you are assisting be free from mental, emotional, and physical pain. It is not enough that we just think of healing the physical expression of an illness (if there is one); we must also seek to remove the emotional suffering and, with it, the wrong views or mental habits that are born of ignorance.

If you are physically present, all the better; however, time and space have no significant effect except that physical contact can create a sense of assurance in the patient and confidence in the operator. If you are present, use the following guidelines. If you are not physically present, imagine that you are the person you are working on. Perform the meditation in the first person, but imagine that your consciousness is attuned to the consciousness of the person you are seeking to assist and is inside their body. Do not be surprised if at some point you experience an actual transfer of consciousness.

1. Place your hands over the affected area.

2. As you inhale, imagine the energy leaving the diseased organ, entering your left hand, moving into your heart or solar plexus, and, as you hold your breath, being transformed into brilliant light filled with its corresponding virtue.

3. As you exhale, see the transformed energy exiting through your right hand and entering into the organ vitalizing it.

4. Do this for at least seven minutes. Offer a prayer of thanks and gratitude for your success in this work and the healing it has brought to yourself and others so that you and they may experience Illumination and be a servant and friend of humanity.

Always remember, it is not you who heals, but the divine energy within and around us. We act as joyful and willing conduits to assist in the healing process. When finished doing contact healing, always wash your hands in cold running water and dry them off, and be sure to check that you are fully aware of your place in time and space.

Guides for Daily Living

In addition to the spheres that are associated with planets and are given a virtue and vice as an expression of their daily presence, there is also the sphere of Kingdom (Malkuth), which contains the virtue of discrimination and the vice of inertia; Wisdom (Hokmah), which contains the virtue of devotion; and the Crown (Kether), which contains the virtue of completing the Great Work. Neither of these latter two have a vice, as they exist in a state of unity, or non-duality.

The sphere of Kingdom (Malkuth) represents our day-to-day life, and meditation on its virtue is beneficial in aiding us in making decisions—not just intellectually, but also intuitively. The sphere of Wisdom (Hokmah) can help arouse within us continued aspiration and energy (to overcome the inertia of material life and ego-defeating behaviors), whereas meditation on the Crown center helps us better understand and realize what it means to "complete the Great Work." Through meditation on our Crown center, we bring that reality closer to the surface of our consciousness, rather than viewing it as something to be attained at some distant point in the future. It brings it into the present moment. The more we work with our Crown center, the easier it is to work with the other spheres or their associated planets.

Exercise—The Perfect Practice

Explanation—The Perfect Practice is the simplest, most direct method of healing. It is the summation of all Hermetic and occult truths and methods in a single technique, and it is found in the Hermetic axiom "Think of a thing and you are it."

Type of Practice—This is a core practice and is foundational to all intermediate and advanced occult practices.

Preparation—Prepare in any manner you see fit.

Method—After you have prepared yourself, proceed as follows:

1. Imagine that your body is surrounded by a sphere of brilliant light and that your body is unsubstantial. The light that is glowing out, through, and around you radiates from the center of your self, your heart.

2. Feel the edge of the sphere, your aura, to be firm, clear, and brilliant.

3. Imagine a person who is in need of assistance and who suffers from mental, emotional, or physical illness.

4. Imagine this person clearly, precisely, and in detail, as if standing before you in the sphere of light.

5. Imagine now that you are that person. You see through the eyes, hear through the ears, and sense through the skin of that person.

6. Fill yourself, as this person, with the healing thoughts, feelings, and emotions of health and wholeness that you have created for yourself in previous practices. See the person surrounded by the sphere of brilliant light, which is radiating from the heart. All the time, imagine that you have ceased to exist and have for all practical purposes exchanged places with the person you wish to assist. You are inside their body and mind, experiencing life as they do, but radiating a profound healing energy through their heart.

7. After several minutes, end the practice and offer a prayer of thanks and gratitude for your success in this work and the healing it has brought to yourself so that you may experience Illumination and be a servant and friend of humanity.

Incorporation into Daily Practice—This practice can be done as often as is needed. It is only limited by the ingenuity of the adept who wishes to practice it.

Key Points

- The element of fire is most important, as it gives life and consciousness to our Being.
- Energy (fire) is extracted from the oxygen (air) we breathe and transferred to our blood, lymph, and other endocrine secretions (water), wherein the material body (earth) is built up.

- The element of fire is found in the navel, solar plexus, and heart. By increasing the amount of fire energy in the psychic heart, we harmoniously and directly affect all of our other psychic centers and awaken the Secret Fire, or kundalini.

- The Inner Master, or sense of self as a spiritual being, is encountered in the heart. This experience is often called "Knowledge and Conversation with the Holy Guardian Angel."

- Respect and gratitude for those who came before us in the tradition and preserved it during dark and difficult times is essential in order to truly attune to the teachers and teachings that the Hermetic tradition presents through the tools of alchemy, Kabbalah, and astrology.

- Only through a sincere and heartfelt gratitude can we awaken to our Inner Master, through whom we can transmute all evils, poison, sins, and illness into healing energies.

- All spiritual growth is moral and ethical growth. Spirituality cannot be separated from morality and ethics.

Assignments for Chapter 7

1. List ten things, people, relationships, or experiences for which you are grateful. Do this every night for one month, even if the list repeats itself. Look up the word *gratitude* in several dictionaries and meditate on its root meaning.

2. Make a list of the virtues and vices of each sphere of the Tree of Life and identify your areas of strength and weakness.

3. Pay attention to your emotional reaction to circumstances, events, and people. Identify why you respond the way you do to one of the spheres on the Tree of Life. Work to correct negative reactions with either positive or indifferent ones. Develop positive indifference toward all things you may experience. This focal point of positive indifference is what allows us to heal difficult situations and illnesses within ourselves and others. Along with positive indifference

comes the development of the power of forgiveness. They go hand in hand.

4. Perform the exercises in this chapter and carefully note your responses to them as your practice of them develops and becomes refined.

Closing Thoughts

The future of energetic healing, particularly as it applies to Hermeticism, is an open one. Hermeticism as a whole has several significant barriers it must overcome as a movement if it is to make the same impact in the twenty-first century that it did in the sixteenth and nineteenth centuries. One of the most significant aspects of Hermeticism is that it is synthetic in nature. That is, it seeks out, absorbs, and digests new ideas and makes them a seamless part of its continuation. There is every reason to believe that as we progress, technology in some form will play an even more important part in Hermetic energetic healing. This modern form of alchemy will no doubt involve the ideas of the New Age movement and test them using the scientific model. Advances in physics, psychology, endocrinology, and linguistics will play a significant role in advancing the Hermetic model, even if it is not so named.

Hermeticism and Technology

Perfect examples of this are the scientific studies on homeopathy, prayer, mass telepathy, and possibly even radionics. Radionics is a strange form of energetic healing that combines talismanic, sympathetic, planetary, and natural magic with sacred geometry and dresses it up in technological garb. According to many people, it works very well.

As we progress, we will realize that there is no such thing as "natural" and "unnatural," there are only energies we understand and use and those we don't.

This is not new to Hermeticism. From its revival in the Renaissance, Hermeticism has always been concerned with three things: (1) establishing an overarching philosophical and theoretical framework to unify the arts and sciences; (2) establishing a verifiable means whereby individuals could directly access the invisible realms without the need of an intermediary; and (3) universal reformation, or the establishment of a society that encouraged and supported the first two points. Much of the "utopian" literature of the West comes from this period or is directly influenced by it.

As we move into the Age of Aquarius—a technological sign and one concerned with social reformation—many of the ideals held by the Renaissance Hermeticists and their later followers have been and will be accomplished, although not without their own problems as well.

While there is much talk of multiculturalism and cross-culturalism, it is important to remember that individual cultures are significant to this work. All esoteric systems reflect the culture out of which they have grown and which they seek to serve. Ignoring the cultural context of a teaching is like studying the mineral content of a plant and never examining the soil it grew in. Just as modern family dynamics stress the roles each person plays in a healthy or dysfunctional family, so too does the culture act as a larger family unit, impacting the development of the individual or of smaller family and tribal units.

Hermeticism: Synthetic or Eclectic?

Even a superficial study of esotericism, be it from any tradition, time, or place, will reveal that systems grow upon and off of one another. The Egyptian deities rose from being local gods and goddesses to being the focus of national and even international cults. Buddhism adapted itself to whatever culture it was brought into, and, in the instance of Tibet, it absorbed many of the existing cultural practices into itself and its various schools. Even Christianity, with its attempts at being a doctrinal and ritualistic monolith, has over the course of its lifespan been based on previous traditions—Jewish and classical—and has incorporated various Nordic and Celtic practices into its fold from time to time.

Hermeticism is clearly a synthetic tradition, in that it has absorbed, digested, and assimilated the theory and practice of several schools into a coherent whole. This was first done during the period of Alexandrian Hermeticism (first century AD), again during the Renaissance (fourteenth to sixteenth centuries), and again during the European Occult Revival. As such, there is every reason to believe that it will continue to do this again and again.

However, the distinction between a synthetic system and an eclectic one must be clearly drawn out. Eclecticism is an approach, not a system, and while it is fine for those who wish to experiment in a wide area of topics to gain experience, it cannot provide the same consistency or level of return as a demonstrated system. A system has a central framework and philosophic core; it has integrated branches and subsets as well as a beginning, middle, and end. That is, it has a specific purpose for being and evolving that is demonstrated by its past and current practitioners. Eclecticism cannot offer that, as it is always in a process of development and reflects the consciousness solely of its owner-developer.

This is stated so that students of Hermeticism or Hermetic Kabbalah are clear on what a developed system can offer them. Understanding this makes it imperative that they examine what they are trying to get out of their esoteric practices. Only when we possess mental clarity of and emotional congruity with our goals can they be achieved.

The Great Challenge to the Traditions

The challenge of modern esotericism as a whole is for it to be a living and vibrant tradition and not simply an exercise in publishing. Spiritual authors must first and foremost be exponents of the methods they preach and, in that, be morally and ethically upright and reliable. They must be able to demonstrate that esotericism is a meaningful contribution to their lives and can be so for anyone who undertakes its journey.

Authors also need to write and teach in a manner that makes the many rich traditions of Western esotericism accessible, meaningful, and practical. It does no good if a tradition exists and no one knows about it, nor does it do any good to know about it if it is incomprehensible. Plain and simple language without reliance on specialized terms demonstrates mastery of the topic. If you can't explain it to my grandmother or someone with an eighth-grade education, then chances are you don't really understand the material. It is an abstraction and not a concrete tool.

Moreover, the methods presented must demonstrate that they make a person's life better in practical, everyday terms. Too many would-be magicians are morally bankrupt or emotionally immature, staining the teachings through their weakness. It always seems that it is they who shout the loudest, creating the impression that they speak for everyone when they do not.

Yet despite this, the future for the traditions of Western esotericism is wide open and is a bright one in many respects. May each who read *Kabbalah for Health & Wellness* have the opportunity to demonstrate to themselves, and maybe a close friend or two, the value of traditional esotericism in daily living, and thereby add to the glory of the living, practical Hermetic tradition.

Finis

Glossary

Ain Soph Aur—The Limitless Light of Kabbalah. This is the primordial Void from which everything has come and to which it will return.

Air—Through correspondence, air expresses and rules all gases, the nervous system, and organizational abilities and acts as a balance and buffer between the extremes of fire and water.

Alchemy—The art and science of creating medicines from plants and minerals for healing physical and psychic diseases, thereby restoring the alchemist to a state of perfect harmony. These medicines can be either liquid, such as the Elixir of Life, or solid, such as the Philosopher's Stone. Alchemy is also known as the Royal Art.

Astral—A state of consciousness in which the physical expressions of life and consciousness are imbued with a transpersonal energy and hyper-reality; inversely, abstract mental and spiritual ideas are clothed with concrete forms, creating what are called archetypes. The so-called astral plane is an expression of the various states of consciousness that can be expressed and encountered during deep meditation, lucid dreaming, and astral projection. These states are created similarly to how the various colors of the spectrum are formed when light encounters a prism.

Astrology—The art and science of charting the impact of cycles on human consciousness and matter. Twelve signs are used to describe the major functions of each cycle, with each sign having a ruling planet as well as an elemental attribute. The various parts of the human body are assigned rulership by a particular astrological sign, whereas the entire person is influenced by the birth sign. A sampling of the astrological signs and their areas of influence in the human body include: Aries—face and head; Taurus—neck, shoulders, and arms; Gemini—lungs; Cancer—stomach, breasts, and womb; Leo—heart and blood; Libra—liver; Virgo—back; Scorpio—intestines and sexual organs; Sagittarius—hips and thighs; Capricorn—knees; Aquarius—kidneys, bladder, and ankles; Pisces—legs as a whole, and feet in particular.

Correspondences—A method of assigning meaning and interdependent connections to the various aspects of the visible and invisible worlds wherein each color, sound, metal, plant, animal, organ of the human body, and anything else in the material world is said to have its origin in the invisible through specific energetic signatures. Astrology plays a significant role in assigning and deciding correspondences.

Cube of Space—A model, found in the *Sepher Yetzirah*, of how the invisible energies expressed by the Hebrew alphabet interact with one another to create the invisible worlds.

Divine Names—Names, or more correctly titles of God, used in Kabbalah and most schools of ritual magic to invoke divine energies of a specific and highly tuned nature into the work being performed. These names are pronounced in a manner that creates a distinct vibration in the body of the operator, and often the environment, and they are critical to most magical operations.

Earth—Through correspondence, earth expresses and rules all solid, hard, and distinctly physical things, including the senses as a whole, and is the foundation for the three remaining elements. Everything comes to rest on the solidity of earth.

Elements—The four primary expressions of energy in the material world: earth, water, air, and fire.

Elixir Vitae—The alchemical Elixir of Life, said to be able to heal all illness and disease as well as to extend human life.

Emerald Tablet—A tablet upon which is said to have been written the famous Hermetic axiom "As above, so below." The Emerald Tablet contains the entire teachings of Hermeticism in a single paragraph.

Etheric—A complex substratum of energy and intelligence that gives rise to material form and maintains it. The etheric is interconnected with the subconscious mind, our instincts, and physical matter itself. The etheric body or matrix is critical in physical healing, transformational operations in alchemy, and all areas of natural magic.

Fire—Through correspondence, fire expresses and rules all forms of energy, particularly dynamic and powerful energy, heat, and light. Fire is individualized consciousness and is the chief animating force in the material and psychic worlds. Fire is the seed of consciousness and life.

Flashing Sword—A term given for Mezla, or the descent of divine energy down the Tree of Life from the Nothingness (Ain Soph Aur) to material form.

Four—The number four relates to the idea of perfect form and material expression.

Hermes—A name given to Thoth, the Egyptian lunar god of magic, taken from the Greek god bearing the same name who acted as the "messenger of the gods."

Hermeticism—The main school of esoteric thought in Western Europe from the Renaissance onward. Hermeticism is rooted in the first century AD and is a synthesis of Gnosticism, remnants of the Egyptian mystery schools, Platonism, and Christianity. It is called an "art and science" in that alchemy, astrology, and Kabbalah are its principal practical expressions.

Kabbalah—A school of Jewish mysticism appearing in the tenth and eleventh centuries, with roots in early mystical systems. Several schools of Kabbalah exist, the most popular using one or more variations of the Tree of Life.

Karma—The primary law of creation, stating that all actions are causes that have effects, which in turn become causes themselves. This relationship of action and reaction, cause and effect, is the basis for all interactions of consciousness and life. Only by understanding that law of karma do we understand the nature of creation and see that all experiences we have are self-created. Karma is the universal scales of balance, or universal justice. As a result of karma, each of us is responsible for our own condition in life—and our own Becoming as a spiritual being.

Klippoth—Fragmented and chaotic energies existing on a macrocosmic and microcosmic level that must be integrated for complete healing and spiritual Illumination to take place. The klippoth are very difficult to deal with directly and are often addressed only in advanced practices.

Levels of the Soul—In Kabbalah, the soul, or consciousness, is stated as expressing itself at four distinct levels. These are as follows: *Guph*—physical body; *Nephesh*—etheric or instinctual level; *Ruach*—the rational mind or objective consciousness; *Neshamah*—spiritual consciousness. These levels of the soul correspond to the Four Worlds.

Magic—The utilization of symbols, often in complex formulas or rituals, to affect consciousness and matter in accordance with a predetermined and specific outcome.

Mezla—The flow of energy, consciousness, and matter through its various phases of expression in the Tree of Life, from the subtle unity of the absolute to the dense realm of matter.

Natural Magic—A system of magic that relies heavily on correspondences, astrological cycles, and planetary hours. The name "natural magic" appears for the first time in the Renaissance, when students of magic wanted to distinguish this practice from "Angelic" and "Demonic" magic.

Path of Return—The reversal of the flow of Mezla, or the ascent of energy and consciousness from matter to the subtle spiritual realms. This is also known as the *Path of the Serpent*.

Paths—Specific connecting links on the Tree of Life that unite two distinct areas of consciousness and matter, thereby forming a synthesis for increased function and clarity. Paths are undertaken in a formal manner wherein, through their activation, interior integration is heightened, physical health improved, and psychic powers enhanced.

Planets—The seven ancient planets, or planets visible to the eye, are traditionally given influence over specific expressions of consciousness, material form, and energies of life both inside and outside of the physical body. In addition, they are used to represent the expression of subtle psychic energies, and each is related to a psychic center as well as a day of the week. This connection of the planets to the psychic centers and cyclic flow or energy as demonstrated across the week gives rise to the use of planetary hours in operations of natural magic.

Planetary Hours—Periods of time that divide each day, from sunrise to sunrise, into "hours" in which specific planetary energies are dominant. Planetary hours are used extensively in alchemy and talismanic magic. Several systems of charting the planetary hours exist.

Prayer—A form of inner dialogue or conversation with the universal mind. This can be formal or informal and can be directed to the Godhead, an angelic being, one's own Holy Guardian Angel, or the Inner Self.

Psychic Centers (Chakras)—Locations in the etheric body that allow for the exchange of energy and information between the subtle psychic consciousness and the physical body, as well as between the psychic and spiritual aspects of consciousness and the rational mind.

Ritual—A prearranged formal use of symbols to convey a point or to create an environment in which specific psychic and/or physical phenomena will take place.

Secret Fire—The etheric energy that underlies all material form. The Secret Fire is influenced by thoughts, feelings, and astrological cycles and can be directed by the focused imagination as well as the use of correspondences in operations of magic. This is identical to kundalini in Eastern yoga.

The *Sepher Yetzirah* (Book of Formation)—One of the oldest and most important books of Jewish mysticism, in which the various relationships of the Hebrew letters to the psychic and material worlds are described. The Tree of Life and the Cube of Space are outlined therein. The *Sepher Yetzirah* is more of a shorthand meditation manual than an actual written thesis.

Sephirah—A single sphere or level of the Tree of Life. The Tree of Life is composed of ten *Sephiroth* (plural), often simply called spheres. These spheres are focal points of energy, matter, and consciousness and represent the major functions, laws, and expressions of creation. They have both archetypal existence and distinct relationships within the individual's psychic body. The spheres are as follows: Kether—cranium; Hokmah—left side of head; Binah—right side of head; Chesed—left shoulder; Geburah—right shoulder; Tiphareth—heart and torso; Netzach—left hip; Hod—right hip; Yesod—sexual organs; and Malkuth—feet and the body as a whole.

Sphere of Sensation—A term used in Western magical systems derived from the Hermetic Order of the Golden Dawn for the energy "egg" or "sphere" that surrounds living beings. It is often used interchangeably with the term "aura," although there are some specific functions of the Sphere of Sensation that are not normally described in relation to the aura.

Talismanic Magic—A system of magic that uses material objects to collect and hold etheric and astral energies, based on the Doctrine of Correspondences, to assist in the actualization of predetermined and specific material or psychic operations and their intended material and/or psychic effects.

Tetragrammaton—*Tetragrammaton* is Greek and means "four-lettered name." It is considered unpronounceable and is the source of all divine power in Kabbalah. Each letter has a particular association with one of the Four Worlds, an element, and a general location in the human body. Changing the order of the letters produces other divine names—all of the same essential power but each with a unique emphasis—that are associated with the twelve signs of the zodiac, the twelve tribes of Israel, the twelve apostles, and the twelve major personality types of humanity. Some modern scholars pronounce it as "Yahweh"; early Christians, as "Jehovah."

Water—Through correspondence, water expresses and rules all forms of liquids, as well as emotions and sensitivities both psychic and physical. Water is the material expression of the energies of life.

Worlds—Levels of consciousness existing in complex relationships with each other. They are: *Assiah*—the material world from the smallest atom to the outermost edges of the universe; *Yetzirah*—the astral world, or subtle energy patterns of the collective consciousness in which a sense of individuality still predominates; *Briah*—the World of Archetypes, wherein the individuality is progressively eclipsed by the Self; *Atziluth*—the spiritual world of pure unity.

Selected Bibliography

Aggripa, Henry Cornelius. *Three Books of Occult Philosophy.* Translated by James Freake (1651). Edited and annotated by Donald Tyson. St. Paul, MN: Llewellyn, 1993.

Ashcroft-Nowicki, Dolores. *Illuminations: Mystical Meditations on the Hebrew Alphabet.* St. Paul, MN: Llewellyn, 2003.

Bardon, Franz. *Initiation into Hermetics.* Wuppertal, Germany: Dieter Ruggeberg, 1987.

Braden, Gregg. *The Isaiah Effect: Decoding the Lost Science of Prayer and Prophecy.* New York: Harmony Books, 2000.

Cicero, Chic, and Sandra Tabatha Cicero. *Self-Initiation into the Golden Dawn Tradition.* St. Paul, MN: Llewellyn, 1995.

Dubuis, Jean. *Fundamentals of Esoteric Knowledge.* Lessons 1–12. Winfield, IL: Triad Publishing, 1996. (Sample lessons available online at http://www.triad-publishing.com/Course_eso.html.)

———. *Qabala.* Lessons 1–72, 3 vols. Winfield, IL: Triad Publishing, 1996. (Sample lesson available online at http://www.triad-publishing.com/Course_qbl.html.)

Fortune, Dion. *The Cosmic Doctrine.* York Beach, ME: Weiser, 2000.

———. *The Mystical Qabalah.* York Beach, ME: Weiser, 2000.

Fortune, Dion, and Gareth Knight. *The Circuit of Force.* Loughbrough, UK: Thoth Publications, 1998.

Gerber, Richard. *Vibrational Medicine: New Choices for Healing Ourselves.* Santa Fe, NM: Bear & Co., 1996.

Gilbert, R. A. *The Golden Dawn Scrapbook: The Rise and Fall of a Magical Order.* York Beach, ME: Weiser, 1997.

Haralick, Robert M. *The Inner Meaning of the Hebrew Letters.* Northvale, NJ: Jason Aronson, Inc., 1995.

Herr, Karl. *Hex and Spellwork: The Magical Practices of the Pennsylvania Dutch.* York Beach, ME: Weiser, 2002.

Jacobi, Jolande, ed. *Paracelsus: Selected Writings.* Bollingen Series XXVIII. Princeton, NJ: Princeton University Press, 1951.

Kaplan, Aryeh. *Sefer Yetzirah: The Book of Formation; In Theory and Practice.* York Beach, ME: Weiser, 1993.

Mead, G. R. S. *Thrice Greatest Hermes: Studies in Hellenistic Theosophy and Gnosis.* York Beach, ME: Weiser, 2001.

Moore, Thomas. *The Planets Within: The Astrological Psychology of Marsilio Ficino.* Hudson, NY: Lindisfarne Press, 1990.

Regadie, Israel. *A Garden of Pomegranates: Skrying on the Tree of Life.* St. Paul, MN: Llewellyn, 2002.

———. *The Art of True Healing.* Edited by Marc Allen. Novato, CA: New World Library, 1991.

———. *The Middle Pillar.* 3rd ed. Edited and annotated by Chic Cicero and Sandra Tabatha Cicero. St. Paul, MN: Llewellyn, 1970.

———. *The One Year Manual.* York Beach, ME: Weiser, 1981.

Roney-Dougal, Serena. *Where Science and Magic Meet.* Rockport, MA: Element Books, 1991.

Schrödter, Willy. *Commentaries on the Occult Philosophy of Agrippa.* York Beach, ME: Weiser, 2000.

———. *The History of Energy Transference: Exploring the Foundations of Modern Healing.* York Beach, ME: Weiser, 1999.

Shulman, Jason. *Kabbalistic Healing: A Path to an Awakened Soul.* Rochester, VT: Inner Traditions, 2004.

Suares, Carlo. *The Cipher of Genesis: The Original Code of the Qabala as Applied to the Scriptures.* York Beach, ME: Weiser, 1992.

———. *The Second Coming of Reb YHSHWH: The Rabbi Called Jesus Christ.* York Beach, ME: Weiser, 1994.

Three Initiates. *The Kybalion: Hermetic Philosophy*. Chicago: Yogi Publication Society, 1940.

White, David Gordon. *The Alchemical Body: Siddha Traditions in Medieval India*. Chicago: The University of Chicago Press, 1996.

White, John, ed. *Kundalini, Evolution and Enlightenment*. Garden City, NY: Anchor Books, 1979.

Zalewski, Pat. *Kabbalah of the Golden Dawn*. St. Paul, MN: Llewellyn, 1993.

Index

Free Magazine

Read unique articles by Llewellyn authors, recommendations by experts, and information on new releases. To receive a **free** copy of Llewellyn's consumer magazine, *New Worlds of Mind & Spirit,* simply call 1-877-NEW-WRLD or visit our website at www.llewellyn.com and click on *New Worlds.*

🌙 LLEWELLYN ORDERING INFORMATION

Order Online:
Visit our website at www.llewellyn.com, select your books, and order them on our secure server.

Order by Phone:
- Call toll-free within the U.S. at 1-877-NEW-WRLD (1-877-639-9753). Call toll-free within Canada at 1-866-NEW-WRLD (1-866-639-9753)
- We accept VISA, MasterCard, and American Express

Order by Mail:
Send the full price of your order (MN residents add 6.5% sales tax) in U.S. funds, plus postage & handling to:

Llewellyn Worldwide
2143 Wooddale Drive, Dept. 0-7387-0977-8
Woodbury, MN 55125-2989, U.S.A.

Postage & Handling:

Standard (U.S., Mexico, & Canada). If your order is:
$24.99 and under, add $3.00
$25.00 and over, FREE STANDARD SHIPPING

AK, HI, PR: $15.00 for one book plus $1.00 for each additional book.

International Orders (airmail only):
$16.00 for one book plus $3.00 for each additional book

Orders are processed within 2 business days.
Please allow for normal shipping time. Postage and handling rates subject to change.

The Path of Alchemy

Energetic Healing and the World of Natural Magic

MARK STAVISH

Alchemy offers tremendous insight into alternative therapies, new medicines, and the depths of the human mind. Illuminating a truly esoteric practice, Mark Stavish reveals how to create and apply "medicines for the soul" in this remarkable guide to plant and mineral alchemy.

The Path of Alchemy introduces the history and basic laws of this ancient practice, and explains how it ties into Qabala, tarot, astrology, and the four elements. Safe, modern techniques—based on spagyrics (plant alchemy)—for producing distillations, stones, tinctures, and elixirs are given, along with their uses in physical healing, spiritual growth, psychic experiments, initiation, consecration, spellwork, and more. Each chapter includes meditations, projects, and suggested reading as aids to "inner transformation," an equally important aspect of alchemy. Tools, rituals, lunar and solar stones, and the elusive Philosopher's Stone are all covered in this comprehensive guide to alchemy.

0-7387-0903-4
288 pp., 6 x 9 $14.95

Simplified Qabala Magic

TED ANDREWS

The mystical Qabala is one of the most esoteric yet practical systems for expanding your consciousness and unfolding your spiritual gifts. Within its Tree of Life lies a map to the wisdom of the ancients, the powers of the universe and to ourselves. As the earliest form of Jewish mysticism, it is especially suited to the rational Western mind.

The Qabala has traditionally been presented as mysterious and complex. *Simplified Qabala Magic* offers a basic understanding of what the Qabala is and how it operates. It provides techniques for utilizing the forces within the system to bring peace, healing, power, love, and magic into your life.

0-7387-0394-X
240 pp., 5³⁄₁₆ x 8   **$9.95**

To Write to the Author

If you wish to contact the author or would like more information about this book, please write to the author in care of Llewellyn Worldwide and we will forward your request. Both the author and publisher appreciate hearing from you and learning of your enjoyment of this book and how it has helped you. Llewellyn Worldwide cannot guarantee that every letter written to the author can be answered, but all will be forwarded. Please write to:

Mark Stavish
℅ Llewellyn Worldwide
2143 Wooddale Drive, Dept. 0-7387-0977-8
Woodbury, MN 55125-2989, U.S.A.
Please enclose a self-addressed stamped envelope for reply,
or $1.00 to cover costs. If outside U.S.A., enclose
international postal reply coupon.

Many of Llewellyn's authors have websites with additional information and resources. For more information, please visit our website at:

www.llewellyn.com